Preaching Eyes
For
Listening Ears

Sermons And Commentary For Preachers And Students Of Preaching

J. Will Ormond

Introduction and Commentary by
Lucy A. Rose

Preface by
Thomas G. Long

CSS Publishing Company, Inc., Lima, Ohio

Copyright © 1999 by
CSS Publishing Company, Inc.
Lima, Ohio

Scripture quotations are from the *Revised Standard Version of the Bible,* copyrighted
1946, 1952 ©, 1971, 1973, by the Division of Christian Education of the National Council of the Churches of Christ in the USA. Used by permission.

Library of Congress Cataloging-in-Publication Data

Ormond, J. Will, 1919-
    Preaching eyes for listening ears : sermons and commentary for preachers and stu-
dents of preaching / J. Will Ormond : introduction and commentary by Lucy A. Rose :
preface by Thomas G. Long.
        p.   cm.
    ISBN 0-7880-1320-3 (pbk.)
    1. Preaching. I. Rose, Lucy Atkinson, 1947-1997.   II. Title.
BV4211.2.O75   1999
252—dc21   98-48038
                                                                                CIP

This book is available in the following formats, listed by ISBN:
        0-7880-1320-3   Book
        0-7880-1321-1   Disk
        0-7880-1322-X   Sermon Prep

PRINTED IN U.S.A.

*This volume is dedicated
to
the memory of
my colleague
Lucy Atkinson Rose
February 15, 1947 — July 17, 1997
without whose persistent encouragement
this collection of sermons
would never have been gathered together.*

Table Of Contents

Preface

To read these sermons is first of all and most of all to hear a voice. The sermons in this book have necessarily become ink on paper, but they are not captive to the printed page. This distinctive voice belongs, of course, to J. Will Ormond, for many years Professor of Biblical Exposition at Columbia Theological Seminary in Decatur, Georgia, and, before that, a longtime pastor of Presbyterian churches in Marion and Tuscaloosa, Alabama. Whenever Will Ormond preached in the Columbia Seminary chapel, the pews were packed with students, colleagues, and often people from the larger community as well, all eager to hear this enchanting and witty voice and to discover what sermonic wonders would be displayed this day.

Will Ormond's popularity as a preacher, both in seminary and congregational settings, is no surprise. To hear his voice in the pulpit is an unforgettable experience. Widely hailed as a superb preacher, he does not boom with the orator's bass, but allows his reedy tenor to caress each well-chosen word. Where some preachers would shout like a parent, Will Ormond whispers playfully like a gently mischievous friend; where some preachers would stare a congregation down, he arches an eyebrow and winks conspiratorially; where some preachers issue demands, he spins winsome yarns, his words as warm and inviting as a southern river on a lazy summer day. In the pulpit, Will Ormond is the gracious and whimsical uncle all of us wish we had, a merry and gentle sprite teasingly poking the ribs of our imagination.

The reason Will Ormond has a welcome voice is that he also has a discerning eye. Before he speaks, he sees. He can see humor in the drab landscapes of daily routine; he can see wisdom in neglected nooks and crannies of biblical texts; he can see imaginative and innovative sermon possibilities where others find only the prosaic and the predictable. Most of all, he can see the gospel, its graces and its demands, and because he sees, he speaks with strong courage, sharp wit, compelling images, refreshing language, and deep faith.

We are fortunate to have this collection of fine sermons from the pen — more accurately, from the tongue — of J. Will Ormond. The excellent commentary of his colleague at Columbia Theological Seminary, homiletician Lucy Rose, helps those of us who read these sermons not only to be moved by them but also to learn from them.

So, read the sermons with pleasure and profit, but also listen, listen, for that wonderful voice.

Thomas G. Long
Princeton Theological Seminary

Introduction

These sermons should first be read devotionally, prayerfully, with an ear and a heart tuned to hear the gospel that is sounded so poignantly and faithfully again and again. Or, to shift the metaphor, each of these sermons is a jewel, finely cut by a master craftsman. We do well to pause and watch the radiance that flickers across each many-faceted surface and that sparkles deep within the gem's heart. We do well to let that radiance first find its reflection in our own hearts and in our lives. Then — once the sermons have cast their spell, strengthening our faith and challenging us to fresh commitment — then they warrant a second reading, and a third, for they have much to teach about sermon form and sermon-making.

Studying these sermon shapes and gathering clues about sermon composition can help both students of preaching and seasoned preachers improve their sermon-making. Here are examples of some of the various forms that are championed by homiletical scholars — story, narrative,[1] deductive, inductive. I invite students who are searching for their own preaching style and pastors who are hoping to expand their repertoire of sermon forms to take a second and a third look at these sermons.

Take any collection of items and there will always be a variety of ways to classify and describe them. I am a wildflower enthusiast. I spend hours of vacation time scouring forest floors, meadows, and roadsides for wildflowers. I love recognizing familiar ones and calling them by name, as though they were old friends. I sketch unfamiliar ones, take notes, and flip through my books in search of new names. And, when I find one, I add it to my "life list," as though I were registering its name in a guest book, or perhaps more accurately, adding its name to my registry of those homes in which I have visited. Over the years I have collected a number of books that categorize and describe selected wildflowers. Several arrange the flowers by color — a section for yellow flowers, another for white, another for red, and so on. Others arrange the flowers by families, sometimes with a key to help with identification — for example, "corolla and calyx present; fruit 2-seeded" or "corolla present; calyx absent; fruit 1-seeded."[2]

My classifications and descriptions of Ormond's sermons are idiosyncratic. My interest is in sermon form and in identifying characteristics of particular sermon shapes. These sermons could be classified just as easily according to content, or exegetical method, or preaching context. Even my classifications here according to form are open to revision because, unlike wildflowers, there is no consensus about sermonic colors or families among homiletical scholars.

The set of categories by which I have classified the majority of Ormond's sermons reflect standard sermons patterns. Both Thomas G. Long in his textbook *The Witness of Preaching* (1989, pp. 127-129) and Fred B. Craddock in his textbook *Preaching* (1985, p. 177) list a number of such patterns that have served preaching well over the years. Ormond has claimed and tailored several of these templates according to his own unique style. The four categories I have used are Story, Problem-Solution, Then-Now, and Now-Then-Now.

I was told when I was learning to preach that it is wise for preachers to have in their quiver a number of tried-and-true patterns like arrows that they can pull out and use on appropriate occasions. Although I am uncomfortable with the image of shooting a sermon at the congregation, I resonate with the idea of having several familiar patterns close at hand like tools in the carpenter's apron or measuring spoons in the kitchen drawer closest to the work counter.

The four patterns described here — Story, Problem-Solution, Then-Now, and Now-Then-Now — are by no means old-fashioned or outdated. Preachers and students of preaching who study Ormond's contemporary and personal use of these patterns may decide to experiment with one or more for their own repertoire, adapting and tailoring them to fit their own unique voices.

In addition to the four categories, a major division that is recognized by a number of homiletical scholars distinguishes between deductive and inductive preaching. Scholars like Fred B. Craddock (1979) and the team of Ralph L. Lewis and Gregg Lewis (1983) have described the differences in detail.[3] Will Ormond's sermons here illustrate these differences. For those who want to experience and observe, evaluate and practice one style, or the other, or both, I have identified three sermons as deductive, selected three inductive sermons, and set them apart for detailed discussion. The discussion of inductive preaching also revisits one of the story-sermons.

Ormond's sermons disprove the misunderstanding that I have regularly encountered, and perhaps have fostered, that a person by disposition or personality structure is either a deductive preacher or an inductive preacher. Ormond is proof positive that the same preacher can adopt first one style, then the other, and faithfully communicate the gospel through both.

The order in which these sermons and their discussions is arranged is first, the story-sermons; then the sermons that illustrate the differences between deductive and inductive preaching; then the sermons that comprise the final three categories of sermons forms. The discussion of the sermon shapes follows the set of sermons.

Lucy A. Rose

Story-Sermons

Luke 1:57-66

Why Can't We Call Him Clarence?

This sermon was first preached in the chapel of Columbia Seminary during Advent, 1972. It was repeated, with very little modification, during Advent in 1981, 1985, and 1993, always by request.

The sermon is centered around the desire of the relatives of the parents of John the Baptist to name the child after his father. This reminded me of how often relatives today suggest names for new babies and are offended when the child is not given a traditional family name.

The sermon shifts the setting into more modern times, and the preacher takes the part of two women, one the mother of the newborn child, the other an imaginary family friend. This is a somewhat unique form of the "first person sermon" because the preacher himself is male.

Two ladies past middle age are sitting in a well-appointed but somewhat old-fashioned parlor having a cup of tea. Let us listen in on their conversation.

"My dear, how nice that after all these years you and Clarence should have a son to carry on the family name and the family business. I don't know how many times I've said to Mortimer, 'What a pity that Clarence and Betty don't have any children. They would make wonderful parents — such fine Christian people, a nice home, a good family background, not to mention a prosperous family business.'

"Mortimer and I wouldn't miss the christening for the world. I understand the bishop himself is going to be here to do it. I haven't heard you say what you are going to name the little fellow, but, of course, everybody knows that you will call him Clarence after his father. After all, Clarence has been a family name for generations, and it would be a shame to break the line.

15

"I happen to know that Clarence's sister, Marjorie, wanted to name one of her two boys Clarence after their grandfather, but since Clarence is the eldest and since it is his name, she thought that he should be the one to pass it along. But when it looked as if Clarence was never going to have a son, I think she wished she had gone ahead and called the second boy Clarence.

"But now that you two do have a son there can still be a Clarence in the next generation."

"But we aren't going to name him Clarence."

"Not going to name him Clarence? But why? What in heaven's name are you going to name him?"

"We are going to name him John."

"John! Every Tom, Dick, and Harry is named John. And there aren't many people named Clarence. And besides, I never heard of anybody on Clarence's side or yours named John — unless you have some rich uncle or cousin or someone whom I've never heard of named John who might leave the child a fortune. In that case you could name him John Clarence and still call him Clarence."

"We aren't going to name him Clarence and we are not going to call him Clarence. His name is John."

"But what does Clarence himself think about it? Surely he wants his only son — and he is not likely to have another — named for him. You know he really wants to call that boy Clarence."

"Here he comes now. Why don't you ask him?"

"Clarence! Clarence, dear. Betty tells me that she is not going to name the baby Clarence. Now tell me truly. What do you want to name him?"

*(Hold up sign reading, "**His name is John.**")*
"Well, I never! Why? Why can't we call him Clarence?"

"You can't call him Clarence because we are not going to name him Clarence. Neither of us ever liked the name very much anyway. But there is a whole lot more to it than that.

"We've done a great deal of thinking about this, in fact. Clarence has done so much thinking that he hasn't said a word since he first knew that we were going to have a baby. We feel there must be some special purpose in our having a son so late in life. Maybe God is trying to tell us something.

"This has really focused our eyes on the future instead of on the past. What kind of world is our John going to be living in? One thing is sure, it will be a lot different from the world we have lived in. And who knows? He may be one who helps make it different, and, we hope, better.

"We want to give him the best we can from our own experience, and we don't want him to forget his family heritage and his roots. But in the nature of things we have to face the fact that he may be on his own before he is out of his teens. How do we know he will want to go into the family business? How do we know what he will want to do with his life? For us, even more than for the usual young parents, this boy represents a whole new generation, the beginning of a new day, a new era.

"I don't mind admitting that we are scared. We wonder if we are up to the responsibility. We really don't know what to expect of that new world our son will be living in. And we aren't likely to be here to guide him through it."

"Well, all that sounds very noble and terribly serious. But I still can't see why we can't call him Clarence. After all, that name is part of the family heritage you say you don't want him to forget."

"Yes, it is, but we don't want him to be just one in a long line of Clarences. We want him to be his own person and make his own name. Maybe we are prejudiced, but we think there is something very special and unique about this child of ours. We think of him as literally a gift from God to us, but we don't want to put our exclusive label on that gift. If he really is special then we must not try to keep him for ourselves, or tie him to the past, or hedge him about with too rigid a family tradition.

"Since he is the symbol of a new generation, a new era, then he has a significance far beyond our narrow family circle. So we are not going to call him Clarence. We are going to give him a new, fresh name — John — a new name for a new day.

"I said that we are scared. But we are also full of joy, and wonder, and hope as well. The whole thing's a miracle, you know. If God can give the gift of new life to Clarence and me, if he can so graciously show us that there is a mysterious new day about to break, then God hasn't given up on this old world.

"I'll have to admit that Clarence and I were having a difficult time keeping up our hope until this baby came along. Everything is changing so rapidly. Nobody seems to care about the old values any more. People do such senseless, cruel things to each other these days. The future was looking so bleak and ominous. We had just about decided that the world had gone mad, and that human beings would keep on killing each other and that there would never be peace in our lifetime. About the only hope we had was that we are old and would soon leave this world anyway. We had just about lived out a normal life span, so what else was there to look forward to?

"But then this baby came along! Then it dawned on us that there is a new generation coming after us. So there must be a new age coming, not simply for us, but for the whole universe as well. So we have this tingling anticipation that this newborn boy of ours — this John — is the first bright streak of a new dawn that is breaking.

"Before he was born Clarence and I were simply waiting for the sun to go down on our lives. But now we can hardly wait for each new day to begin, nor do we fear the setting of the sun. Since God has sent us John, who knows? God may have even greater miracles waiting in the wings. And John will doubtless see them even if we don't. After all, we've had miracle enough."

"Well, my dear, I really must be going. Don't get up. I'll let myself out. Thanks for the tea. I'll have to tell Mortimer the new baby is going to have a brand-new name. I hope I can make him understand why we can't call him Clarence."

Oh, No; Not Again ...

This sermon is a retelling in a contemporary setting of the Parable of the Widow and the Judge. The harsh character of the Judge is exaggerated. The imaginary law clerk is made especially wimpish to highlight the arrogance of the Judge.

The Widow, as in the original parable, is the strongest character in the drama, although outwardly she appears to be the weakest.

This sermon emphasizes the biblical theme of the reversal of roles, and the triumph of faithfulness over human power.

There is a timid, tentative knock on the imposing heavy oak door. But from within there is no answer, only an ominous silence. The lowly law clerk knows that the Judge is hunched in his high-back chair, glowering over his papers, idly punching holes in the blotter on his desk with a letter opener which is as sharp as a razor.

The clerk takes a deep breath and lets it out. He knocks again, this time a little more boldly. This time the volcano behind the door rumbles and stirs, and the clerk thinks he sees a fine white ash sifting through the keyhole.

The voice roars like the sound of many waters, and the windows rattle with the swelling thereof.

"Well, Baxter, what do you want?"

The clerk has heard that tone before, and has quaked before it. But better men than he have been reduced to silence by it.

He remembers the delegation of bishops and moderators, of seminary presidents and executive secretaries, of theologians and preachers, of ethics professors and pastoral counselors. (The biblical department had sense enough not to come, because they already knew the story.)

19

This gaggle of ecclesiastical authority had come to see the Judge last week. They were armed with resolutions, position papers, and petitions. They spoke in well-modulated inflections supported by ample diagrams. They talked about the moral order of the universe, the ground of all being, and the sovereignty of God.

Well, that delegation did not get halfway through their supplications. The Judge snatched the resolutions from the bishop's hand and dropped them into the wastebasket. He pinned the moderator to the wall with a glance as hard and sharp and swift as two javelins of steel. He dismissed the delegation as if they were a confused herd of second-class sheep.

"Don't come to me with your God talk, and your moralisms, and your theological jargon. I am the Judge, and I dispense the law as I see fit. Now, get out!"

So the delegation scattered with their clerical collars turned frontward, and tripping over their cassocks and their academic robes.

No wonder the clerk hesitates to answer the Judge's question when he bellows, "Well, Baxter, what do you want?"

"Your honor, sir," Baxter stammers as he pushes the heavy oak door slightly ajar and slithers into the room. "Your honor, she is here again."

"Who is here again, Baxter? Speak up, man."

"Why, you know, sir. The Widow, the one who has been coming every day — sometimes twice — for the past three weeks. The one who has been trying to get you to order the Rip-Off Life Insurance Company to honor her late husband's policy."

The clerk expects another volcanic eruption which would put Vesuvius to shame. But instead the Judge puts his head down on the desk, pounds the desk lightly with his fists, and wails with a plaintive moan:

"Oh, no, not again ... not again!"

"Yes, your honor, again. I am afraid she is here again."

"Well, don't just stand there. Show her in."

Baxter opens the door and a slight woman, plainly dressed, with a wisp of gray hair falling across her cheek, enters the room. But her eyes are clear; her carriage erect; she walks with a solid step.

20

"Sit down, Madam; sit down. Now, tell me again, what is your problem?"

"Well, your honor, as I have told you a number of times, the Rip-Off Life Insurance Company will not honor the policy on my husband's life. They claim he did not pay the last premium before he died. But I have the cancelled check and their receipt which shows that he paid the premium two weeks before it was due."

"So you have, Madam, so you have."

The Judge reaches for a long, legal-looking paper.

"I will sign a court order immediately directing the Rip-Off Life Insurance Company to pay the policy in full. And wouldn't you like to sue them for the mental distress they have caused you?"

Baxter can hardly stifle a gasp, for he knows that the Judge is a heavy stockholder in the Rip-Off Insurance Company.

"No, I do not wish to sue. I want only what is due me."

"And that is what you shall have, Madam; that is what you shall have before this week is out," says the Judge as he gently but firmly guides her toward the door.

"That is all I ever asked for," says the Widow with dignity, "and I am glad at last to have it."

As the woman disappears down the corridor, the Judge goes back to his chambers. Before he slams the door and sinks into his high-back chair, he bellows out to Baxter, "Baxter, bring me a double Scotch, and be quick about it."

But before Baxter hurries to do the Judge's bidding, he dashes down the corridor and catches up with the Widow as she is going down the steps. Without a word he takes her arms, turns her toward him, and plants a resounding kiss on her startled lips. Before she can get her breath he is back up the steps and lost in the gloom of the corridor which leads to the heavy oak door.

For you see, the Widow has won, and Baxter knows it. She has won not by force or influence or wisdom or wealth or through powerful friends, for she has none of these. She has won by sheer persistence, by steadfastness, by holding on, by never giving up, by continuing to hope when there seems to be no ground for hope. And all this adds up to faithfulness.

What fear of God or regard for human power could not do, the Widow's persistent faithfulness finally brings about. The Judge himself admits as much.

"And the Lord said, 'Hear what the unrighteous judge says. And will not God grant justice to his chosen ones, who cry to him day and night? Will he delay long in helping them? I tell you, he will quickly grant justice to them.' "

So then, God is not like this Judge. God does not have to be pestered into being merciful or cajoled into hearing us. God never says when he sees us coming, "Oh, no; not again!"

Persistent faithfulness, then, is not a matter of winning a battle with God. It is not a test of wills between us and God to see which will blink first.

Rather we can be persistent in our faithfulness because we know that God is already patient with us and because we believe that God hears us. Therefore, we can trust God even when he seems silent; we can know that God cares for us even when he seems absent; we can count on God even when his ways baffle us.

We may not be able to figure God out by our wisdom or to lay hold on God by our strength. But we can respond to God's faithfulness with our own faithfulness, not to earn a reward, not to make God do something he does not want to do, but to open our hands to receive a gift.

Our God never says when he sees us coming, "Oh, no; not again!"

Rather God says, "Ask, and it will be given you; seek, and you will find; knock, and it will be opened to you."

In that case, our knocking need not be tentative nor timid; nor need it cease at the sound of silence.

Luke 23:13-25

The Cross Of Barabbas

This is an imaginary story with imaginary characters. The story is told through a conversation between a carpenter and his young apprentice as they construct crosses to be used in a crucifixion. The carpenter is the only one whom we hear speak. The words of the other characters are reflected in the carpenter's responses to them.

The purpose of the sermon is to seek to draw the hearers into the reality of the crucifixion of Jesus by imagining the emotions stirred up in the hearts of some of the people who were there. It also seeks to suggest how both the life and the death of Jesus affected the lives of people with whom he came in contact.

The sermon does not claim to be historically correct insofar as the construction of crosses in the first century is concerned. The first sentence is designed to make that clear.

This sermon was first preached on Good Friday, 1951, in Tuscaloosa, Alabama, while I was pastor of the Covenant Presbyterian Church in the city. It has also been preached in the chapel of Columbia Seminary.

The story I am about to tell does not accurately reflect how crosses were built in the first century, but it may suggest how we build them now.

Come, go with me to old Jerusalem and stand there beside a builder's door and listen as the carpenter speaks to his helper, a young man named Michael:

Step lively there.

You know these crosses three must needs be finished by the morrow.

The Roman captain gave me certain orders to have them ready by the dawn.

There's no need to smooth and plane the upright piece — just so the timber's strong — just so the cross-arm's steady.

What will it matter to the fools who die upon them if there's a splinter here and there?

Oh, you cannot help but wonder who shall die upon them.

Have you not heard?

It is the leader of that robber band that terrorized the city some weeks back. You remember, Barabbas and his crew.

Some said he meant to start a revolution, but I doubt it. Not Barabbas. That black-hearted knave cares not who sits upon the throne and, though his father was a rabbi, it matters not to him who is the priest, nor why. He's bent on pillage. He'd as leave murder for six shekels as for a silver talent.

So don't waste your time making that cross smooth. That's the cross for Barabbas.

So — you even want the cross of Barabbas to be smooth?

What strange notions you received when you apprenticed in that shop at Nazareth. Each tiny task must be just so. You care not how much of time and tools it may cost me.

Now just last week — that kneading trough the widow near the Fish Gate ordered. All day long you measured, smoothed, and rubbed, and for it picked the best wood in the shop. The task — for her — could have been finished in an hour's time. (We did well to get a shekel for it.) But one would think that she was Pilate's wife, the pains you took. And now with dawn about to break you want to make Barabbas' cross so smooth.

Well, at last the task is done.

Go, hitch the oxen to the cart, then hurry back and help me load these crosses.

Heave ho, there. Push them farther toward the front. I don't care to lose one on the way and have to stop and pick it up or put my shoulder under it and drag it through the streets like one condemned.

There! They seem secure.

24

The Praetorium's the place they are to go, or so the Roman captain said. Here, hand me that goad! These oxen are as slow as you.

When we return you must rub some tallow on these axles. Never have I heard the wheels give out with such a groaning squeak. It seems they do protest the load. They know full well that they have carried thrice as much with less than half the noise.

While you were gone to hitch the oxen to the cart, a man stopped by the shop and said that lights burned all night long in Annas' house.

A crowd was gathered in his courtyard 'round a fire, and he could hear the servants laughing as he passed, but their laughs seemed not of mirth.

And, he said, a company of soldiers and a crowd moved through the streets from Annas' to Caiaphas' palace after midnight.

And after dawn they wakened Pilate, who came out on the balcony and spoke to them in angry tones.

I wonder if it has aught to do with the executions that take place today. I see not how, for Barabbas and the others have been condemned already, and they shall surely die upon these crosses we have made.

It could not be a trial for someone else, for the court cannot pass judgment in the night. It is against the law.

And yet I wonder what's afoot. I hope there're no more crosses to be built. Although they pay us for them well, and though they take no special pains — or shouldn't — I, myself, had rather make a yoke for oxen or a baby's crib than turn my hand to make a cross.

But building is our business, and we must build what those who pay do ask.

How now? What's this?

How shall we ever push beyond this crowd that presses 'round the proud Praetorium's door? How can we deliver crosses with such traffic in the way?

What ails them? The chant seems "Crucify!"

Oh, no — if there's to be another crucifixion I hope they hire another shop to build the cross, for we have toiled all night on these, and I am tired.

They cry a name. Ah, it is "Barabbas." They shout Barabbas' name. I see it now. They know this is his execution day, and they are so incensed at all his crimes that they clamor for his blood.

Come, let us skirt the crowd and guide the oxen to the back door of the Judgment Hall. For we bring Barabbas' cross, and since it seems he may need it sooner than he thought, we must not delay a customer.

Sir, here are the crosses that you ordered — all three. That one there — the strong, straight, smooth one — my helper made. It is the one we measured for Barabbas.

Did I hear you aright, sir?

Did you say Barabbas will not need it?

Then we have made one cross too many?

(All your careful work, my friend, seems to have been in vain.)

Oh, it shall not be wasted, but shall be used? But, who, sir? Who shall bear Barabbas' cross? Whose crimes are worse than his? Whose heart more black? Whose hands more bloody? What notorious thief takes Barabbas' place upon his cross?

No thief at all, sir? No man with bloody hands? But one whom Pilate said was innocent of any crime? He calls himself a king? A king who is a carpenter? A carpenter from Nazareth?

Michael, did you hear the captain? The man's a carpenter — from Nazareth. Could it be the One from whom you learned the trade? You said he left the shop some three years back. And I have heard of him myself. It's strange things they tell of him — of raising the dead and making the lame walk.

And he's the one, I think, who from the Temple drove the money changers out the other day. They say old Caiaphas was aflame with anger after that.

So — Barabbas will go free and this man will die because the people will it so.

Look, Michael, they bring him now.

It is your carpenter! I can tell it by your face. Look, he said he was a king, and now he wears a crown — though it be of thorns. And a robe — but it is old and torn and faded. And the scepter in his hand is but a broken reed — but he's kingly still!

26

His eyes, his eyes! They turn on me! Never have I seen such eyes before — or never have such eyes seen me. They sear my soul!

This man's a carpenter, and somehow I sense he knows how I've dealt with the trade. How could he know? But as he looks upon me, all those times I've patched a broken piece and passed it off for whole, I do remember. The yokes I've made and knew that they would gall the ox because I did not take the time to shape them well. The widows I have overcharged — the sick whose very beds I've taken back because they could not pay the full price on the day. The timbers I have sneaked by night from off my rival's pile of lumber.

And, Michael — your wages. I know it's been a fortnight since you had it, and I said my purse was low. But now I do confess I had it all the while. And never, Michael, have I ever paid you what you really earned. But you were young and from the country, and I did not think you'd know just what the wage should be. But now that your Master Carpenter has looked on me, I think you knew my errors all the while.

Not a word he utters, Michael, as they show him to his cross — the cross you made. You made it for Barabbas, not for him! And yet he takes it almost joyously, it seems, as if it were his own.

Oh what a world is this that will release Barabbas and lead a man like this to death. I see now why Caiaphas could not let him live. He could not bear his eyes upon his shriveled soul.

The scribes, the Pharisees, those hidebound legalists, how could they hope to understand the likes of him?

And vacillating Pilate — sensual and fat — he must please the howling mob and let justice die.

Ah, yes, I know it's heavy. Did we not load it on the cart? And they will make him carry it alone as he takes Barabbas' place. I'm not surprised he stumbles, for look, his back is raw. He's lost much blood already.

Ah, see! They'll make the black Cyrenian take it for him, but when they reach the top of Calvary it will be his again.

There it goes, Michael — the cross we made. But we made it not alone. The whole world made it for him. And as I watch it

27

move up Golgotha — the cross made for Barabbas — the cross carried by the black Cyrenian — the cross for the Christ — I know that it is not Barabbas' cross — nor Simon's — not even Christ's. But that it is in all justice mine. Only by God's mercy is it his.

Oh, Michael, I am glad you made Barabbas' cross so smooth.

Exodus 12:1-8, 13-14, 25-27

A Lamb For A Household

What piqued my imagination in these instructions for the keeping of the Passover was the admonition that if a household was too small for them to eat one lamb, they were to invite the neighbors next door to share the meal with the small household.

I began to imagine how these instructions might work out in daily life. Would it reveal how neighbors got along with each other? If there had been tension between neighbors could the sharing of the lamb bring about reconciliation?

In this sermon the "head" of a Jewish household carries on a conversation with his wife about preparations for Passover. While we never hear the wife speak, it soon becomes apparent that she understands the real significance of Passover far better than does her husband.

A unique characteristic of this sermon is that at two points voices from the rear of the sanctuary read relevant passages of scripture. This is to give the impression of God speaking to the characters in the drama and to the hearers in the service.

This sermon was preached at a communion service in the Columbia Seminary chapel.

If the Passover continued to be celebrated according to the strict rules of the first one, I wonder if tensions about how it ought to be done did not arise in some families. Suppose we listen in on a conversation which might have taken place in a Jewish household a few centuries after the first Passover.

Yes, Miriam, I know that Passover is only a week away. And, yes, I have looked over the year-old lambs. But, no, I have not chosen one yet.

Why? Well, you ought to know why. There are so many rules. It has to be a male; it has to be perfect, without blemish; it has to be a year old.

Hold your tongue, woman! You need not remind me that my flock is not so large but that it is no overwhelming task to pick out all the year-old male lambs. Yes, I do already know how many there are — thirteen. Then why haven't I chosen one yet?

Well, I have to examine them carefully to be sure that the chosen one is whole — none lame, none with a blind eye, none with a cough or with sores beneath his wool. All that takes time. It takes a long time to look through all that wool.

Now you seek to flatter me. All right, I do know my sheep. What if I do give them all names, and what if I do already know which ones are perfect? I am a good shepherd, and I care well for my sheep. Too well, I'd say, for all the year-old males are fat. They are all too big. That's why I've not picked one out yet for Passover. I've been wondering if perhaps I ought to buy a little one from someone else. For how can you and I and those two sons of ours eat a whole lamb on Passover night? Even given Adonijah's appetite we couldn't manage it.

Nine long years it's been since you bore me a child — not even a daughter. If you had not left off child-bearing there would be enough mouths in this house by now to eat one lamb at Passover — maybe two.

Yes, I know the rule — and that's what bothers me. (I see you've conveniently left the scroll open at the proper place.) "A lamb for a household, and if the household is too small for a lamb, then a man and his neighbor next to his house shall take according to the number of persons; according to what each one can eat you shall make your count for the lamb."

"His neighbor next to his house." You know what that means, don't you? Or rather you know whom that means. And I'll not have it. Nathan and his loudmouthed wife, his gossiping mother-in-law, that impudent son, and those two sniveling daughters.

His goats are always straying into our vineyard and eating the vines. We had a row about it just last week. He said I ought to keep the hedges around the vineyard in better repair. And I told him that those half-starved goats of his could eat their way through a double hedge of thorns any day.

And they aren't too keen about how they keep the Law. I've seen his wife picking up sticks and smoke rising from their oven on the Sabbath. I think they cook on the holy day.

And those children. I'll admit that his son, Jonathan, is a sturdy, rather fine-looking lad, but I think he is something of a bully. He seems always to get the better of our Adonijah in a wrestling match. And his daughters are much too bold and forward for their years.

And another thing. I wager that if we did ask them Nathan would insist on bringing his own wine for the Passover table. He's always saying that I serve mine far too soon before it ripens properly. And I know that his wine is so old that it is as strong as vinegar. I'll have no alien cup on my Passover table. If Nathan would come — and I have no intention of asking him — he will drink my kind of wine or he can go thirsty.

I tell you I don't fancy sharing Passover with Nathan and his crew. Passover ought to be a time when a man can gather with his own family and enjoy it and not have to think about the tensions and disruptions and pain that go with life in this world.

Why, of course, we will put the blood on the doorposts and lintel of our house. I know the ritual. We've been doing it for years.

Where will the blood come from? How dense do you think I am, Miriam? The blood will come from the lamb. And, yes, that will mean that the lamb gave up his life for us. You don't think we are going to eat the lamb alive, do you?

Yes, Adonijah will ask me at the Passover feast, "What do you mean by this service?" I know the right words, and I have taught my sons the right questions.

What do you mean there is a difference between knowing the Passover words and truly celebrating the Passover? You have to do the thing right, and that means saying the right words and getting through the proper ceremony.

But what does it *mean*? You know what it means, and you know that I know what it means. Woman, you forget your place. You ask your questions as if you would instruct me.

31

Well, I guess you could say that tension, disruption, and pain were all involved in that first Passover. Our ancestors were surrounded by death that night, and a great cry of grief went up from the land. But it was through that death that release from bondage came for our fathers and mothers and their feet were set on the road to freedom. The blood on the door reminds us of a life given, of blood poured out to turn death away from our door.

I'll grant you all that, but what has it to do with our inviting Nathan and his brood to share the Passover lamb with us?

More questions? You ask me why the Passover came about in the first place and what it did for our people and what it showed about God?

I'll tell you what it showed. It showed that Moses was smarter than Pharaoh any day, and that God cared more about the Israelites than about the Egyptians — and I hope he still does.

Why do you look so shocked? What do you mean I do not understand our people's history?

(The woman fancies herself a rabbi. Next thing I know she will be wanting to speak in the synagogue.)

All right, remind me of what you say I have forgot. What words of Moses would you have me call to mind?

(Reading from back of the room by two voices.)

Voice One:

You are a people holy to the Lord your God; the Lord your God has chosen you to be a people for his own possession, out of all the peoples that are on the face of the earth. It was not because you were more in number than any other people that the Lord set his love upon you and chose you, for you were that fewest of all peoples; but it is because the Lord loves you, and is keeping the oath which he swore to your ancestors, that the Lord has brought you out with a mighty hand, and redeemed you from the land of bondage, from the hand of Pharaoh, king of Egypt.

Voice Two:

*Hear, O Israel: The Lord your God is one Lord, and
you shall love the Lord your God with all your heart,
and with all your soul, and with all your might.*

*You shall not take vengeance or bear any grudge
against the sons of your own people, but you shall love
your neighbor as yourself. I am the Lord.*

So you would remind me that:

God chose our people not because we deserved to be chosen,
but simply because he loves us.

Our reasonable response to that choice is not only love to God
but also love to neighbor — even people like Nathan.

God calls us to be a people united, reconciled to him and to
each other — to be witnesses to and instruments of his
purpose in the world.

You ask how can we be a people united if I will not even recognize my neighbor next door as my brother and his wife as my
sister? You say what does Passover mean to me if I do not see that
the blood on our door and the blood on their door makes us members of the same people, both set free by God's choice.

How can we be witnesses to God's grace and reconciliation to
the nations if I will not be reconciled with the man whose goats eat
my vines and if I cannot live in peace with the family next door?

Miriam, Miriam, you make it too simple — and you make it
too hard. I must go out under the stars and think about all your
questions.

(Reading from back of the room by two voices.)

Voice Two:

*Now the Lord said to Abram, "Go from your country
and your father's house to the land that I will show
you. And I will make of you a great nation, and I will
bless you and make your name great, so that you will
be a blessing ... By you shall all the families of the earth
bless themselves.*

33

Voice One:

> *The word of the Lord came to Abram ... "Fear not, Abram, I am your shield; your reward shall be very great" ... And he brought him outside and said, "Look toward heaven, and number the stars, if you are able to number them ... So shall your descendants be." And he believed the Lord, and it was reckoned to him as righteous.*

Miriam, the sky is full of the most brilliant stars tonight, and the light of the moon is strangely clear.

I think I will go out to the small sheepfold where I have gathered all the year-old lambs.

Would you call our elder son, Adonijah? Ask him if he would run next door and ask Jonathan, Nathan's son, if he would like to help him choose the Passover lamb from our flock.

There is light enough in this night for them to choose the proper one. And it should be done before the morning comes.

Genesis 2:4-7
Galatians 3:23-29

A Sermon In Clay

This sermon was prepared to be the last in a series of three sermons for the Columbia Forum during the first week of February, 1988. Unfortunately in early January I had emergency open heart surgery and was not sufficiently recovered by the time of the Forum to deliver the sermon.

However, the seminary graciously planned a special service for me to deliver the sermon on the evening of April 12, 1988, when the Board of Directors was on campus. It was the first time I preached after my surgery.

This is a deeply personal true story from my own early childhood. It reflects a relationship between many whites and blacks in the rural Deep South in the first third of the twentieth century which many people have never experienced and which many others do not know.

(This sermon has been published in *A Journal for Preachers*, Easter, 1990, p. 20, and in *In Trust*, Autumn, 1990, p. 25.)

For this sermon I have two texts, one from the Old Testament, and the other from the New.

Genesis 2:7:

> *The Lord God formed Adam of dust from the ground,*
> *and breathed into Adam's nostrils the breath of life;*
> *and Adam became a living being.*

Galatians 3:28, 29:

> *There is neither Jew nor Greek, there is neither slave*
> *nor free, there is neither male nor female; for you are*

all one in Christ Jesus. And if you are Christ's then you
are Abraham's offspring, heirs according to promise.

I was born on a rice farm near Beaumont, Texas, but a few
months before my fourth birthday my parents moved back to their
native Alabama. My father took a job as manager of a large company farm in Sumter County, Alabama.

The three of us lived in a big house with fourteen rooms. The
front yard must have been at least half an acre. On three sides of
the lawn was a concrete retaining wall. You could stand at the highest part of the wall and look down at a row of yucca plants with
their stiff, sharp spikes pointing in all directions. I could imagine
that they were ancient soldiers guarding the battlements with their
spears.

Along the far side of the lawn was a row of two or three catalpa trees. In the evening in late spring or early summer these
trees would be asparkle with tiny points of light as the fireflies
explored the catalpa blossoms.

Although the house was large, it was not an elegant house in
the tradition of Tara or Twelve Oaks. It was a rather plain, severe
house. It seems to me that all the walls inside were gray. It had no
running water, no indoor plumbing, no electricity, and, of course,
no central heat. But most of the other houses that we knew lacked
these things so we did not know we were supposed to miss them.

Along the full length of the house was a wide front porch. This
was a great place for a small boy to run his wheel toys or to sit with
his parents in the evening and watch the fireflies in the catalpa
trees.

The little town where we bought groceries, where we went to
Sunday school and church, and where I started to school, was three
miles away, reached by an unpaved country road which was dusty
when it was dry and muddy when it rained. Our nearest white neighbors lived about a mile down this road toward town.

But we were surrounded by the small houses of the black farm
workers who lived and worked on the place. So my most conve-
nient and frequent playmates were the children from these black
families.

One of them was my special friend. His name was Jethro King Rogers, and he had a particular talent which fascinated me. He could take moist clay and with deft and skillful fingers mold almost anything that he could imagine. He could make horses, cows, dogs, people. He could even make clay automobiles and wagons which turned on clay wheels with sticks for axles. He and I spent hours under the highest part of the house while I watched him make his models and while we played with those which had already dried in the sun.

I was the boss man's son, but all I could make out of the moist clay was mud pies of irregular shape and thickness. In this situation Jethro King Rogers was the creator, but both of us breathed into his models the breath of life with the fantasy with which children endow their toys.

I have often wondered whatever became of Jethro King Rogers. But given the structure of society at the time I am afraid he never had an opportunity to develop his talents beyond making clay toys for himself and his friends.

Life on the farm, at least from my point of view, was slow-paced, calm, and serene, with a wide-open-spaces sense of freedom — and especially it was safe and secure. But all this suddenly changed on one fateful morning. It was as if someone had taken an exquisite cut glass bowl and dropped it on a stone floor where it exploded into a multitude of sharp, shining shards.

It was a warm, cloudless Saturday morning in early May, 1929, less than three weeks after my tenth birthday. My father, as was his custom, had long since left the house to go to the fields to see how the young cotton plants were faring in the dry weather and the warm sun. My mother was sewing brightly colored patches on a pair of my faded bib overalls, and I was watching her with great interest. You see, I was to be in a play at school the next week. I was to play the part of a hobo, and she was making my costume.

Suddenly we heard the running of heavy feet along the wide front porch. One of the farm workers appeared at the door, his eyes wide, his voice tense.

"Mr. Ormond said for you to give me the keys to the car so I can go to town and get Dr. Neil. We found Mr. Ormond sick in the field."

You see, there was no telephone, so the only way to summon the doctor was to go and find him by whatever means of transportation was at hand.

Quickly my mother gave the man the keys, and he was off with a roar of the engine and a cloud of dust. My mother and I ran along the wide front porch, down the concrete steps which pierced the retaining wall and led to the driveway. We ran toward the fields, but before we reached the barns we met a solemn procession.

One farm wagon pulled by two mules with a solemn-faced black man on the driver's seat. On either side of the wagon and behind it came other silent farm workers. On the floor of the wagon, on a bed of hay, lay my father. His eyes were closed. His face was ashen gray. He was ominously still. The wagon stopped. My mother and I climbed into the wagon beside him. We touched his hands. They were cool and clammy. The warm spring air was split with the screams of a young woman who suddenly found herself a widow and the wracking sobs of a ten-year-old boy who knew himself to be among the fatherless. My father was 45 years old.

The procession came to a halt in front of the concrete steps. About that time the doctor arrived. He climbed into the wagon, took out his stethoscope, and placed it on my father's chest. But it was a useless gesture. We all knew that he was dead.

The rest of the day was a confusion of people coming and going, of whispered expressions of sympathy, of offers of "if there is anything that we can do." It was a time of fear, of uncertainty, of despair, and of deep pain. Finally my aunt and uncle arrived from their farm about 25 miles away. He was my father's brother; she was my mother's sister. They enfolded us into their family as if we were quivering birds with broken wings.

The funeral was set for the very next day, a Sunday, at 3:00 in the afternoon. It was to be held at my aunt and uncle's house.

My father's casket rested on two wooden sawhorses in front of the fireplace in the parlor. The lid was open, and there he lay. Still, calm, as if he were asleep. But he did not look real to me. The house soon was filled with the cloying sweetness of florist flowers.

The morning of the day of the funeral I did not know what I was supposed to do with myself. I avoided my mother because I could not bear to see the heartbreak in her eyes or to hear her cry. I wandered aimlessly about the house. I did not know how to deal with the deep, hollow hurt within me. I doubt that I could have identified it as grief. It was more like fear, uncertainty — and even embarrassment. I was already anticipating the questions adults sometimes asked small boys when they weren't sure who they were: "Boy, who's your daddy?"

And I would have to reply, "I don't have a daddy. My daddy's dead."

As the dreaded hour for the funeral approached, I went out on the front porch where a group of men was gathered. Some of them were sitting in wooden benches tilted against the wall. These benches were handmade pews rescued from an abandoned church. There was also a porch swing in which two men sat, swinging gently. That old swing never had been hung properly. If you leaned back in it too far it would tilt over and suddenly and unceremoniously spill you on the porch floor. As I watched the men swinging I almost wished that it would tilt over and break the heavy solemnity of the day. But it never did.

I sat on the front steps and looked out over the pond and the pasture in front of my uncle's house. Then in the distance on the main road I saw a cloud of dust. At first it was no bigger than a person's hand. But as it drew nearer it billowed and grew. It turned off the main road onto the lane that led to my uncle's house. It snaked its way around the little general store which he kept, mostly for the convenience of the workers who lived on his place. It came to a halt in front of the house.

When the dust settled there were two flatbed trucks filled with the black farm workers, both men and women, from the farm where my father had been the boss man. They jumped down and dusted themselves off. They were dressed in their Sunday best.

My uncle went out to greet them. He led them up the walk, up the steps, and opened the door to the hall where I had retreated when I saw them coming. I watched as they passed silently by. Some of their dusty faces were streaked with tears. Some of the women clutched little bunches of wildflowers which they had picked along the fence rows.

I watched as in silent single file they moved into the parlor and passed by my father's open casket. Each one paused for a brief moment of farewell, then they moved back into the front yard and stood together along with a great many other people for whom there was not room in the house.

The service was held in the parlor, and there was room only for relatives and close friends. I remember very little about the service except that a hastily assembled quartet sang two hymns. Now you will not find these hymns in *The Hymnbook,* and they would surely never find their way into the staid and formal *Worshipbook.* I suppose their theology is shallow and naive, and their music does not compare favorably with Bach. They were "Shall We Gather At The River" and "There's A Land That Is Fairer Than Day." Of course, I had never heard the word "eschatological," but somehow those hymns gave me a glimmer of hope — hope that perhaps there was a better day coming even if we had to wait a long time for it — and that maybe God had not completely forgotten us after all.

The service ended. We followed the casket out the front door, down the steps to the waiting hearse. We climbed into cars for the short drive to the old country cemetery about a mile from my uncle's house. The hearse and the lead cars reached the cemetery before the last cars, including the flatbed trucks, left the house. But the graveside service did not begin until all had assembled.

My mother and I and other relatives sat on hard wooden folding chairs set up beside the grave. This was before the days when rural morticians had tents to shield the family from the elements. It was before the days of artificial grass that seeks to mask the deep wound in the earth and to cover the great mound of clay that came from the grave. There it lay, red, raw, and real. It was before the days of mechanical devices which at the touch of the mortician's toe can lower the casket slowly and then stop it before it disappears into the darkness of the earth. Rather, two stout boards were placed across the grave and the casket rested on these. Two strong straps were passed beneath the coffin, and when it was time to lower it the pallbearers and others grasped the straps, made them taut against the bottom of the casket, and lifted it; the boards were taken away, and then the casket was lowered somewhat unsteadily into the depths of the grave.

It was the custom in the rural South in those days for all who had come to the cemetery to remain until the grave was filled, the mound shaped and smoothed, and the flowers placed on the grave. This was part of the ritual, part of the ceremony. It provided a kind of closure to the proceedings. Those who filled the grave considered it an act of devotion and of honor. So when the time came, my father's brothers and other male relatives stepped forward, grasped the shovels, and plunged them into the great mound of clay. But before they could throw the first shovelful a man stepped forward from among the black farm workers who were clustered nearby. For all I know he might have been Jethro King Rogers' father. He reached out a work-hardened hand and said with dignity and compassion, "We would like to do that."

Without hesitation the white men relinquished the shovels to the black men. With efficiency and dispatch they filled the grave. They entombed my father in the good earth to which he and they had been so close, and on which he and they had toiled side by side. They shaped and smoothed the mound. The flowers were placed on the grave.

The ritual, the ceremony, was over. The people began to leave, murmuring to each other in low tones. My mother and I went back to the sanctuary of my aunt and uncle's house. The black farm workers climbed onto their flatbed trucks and headed back to the farm, where tomorrow they would have a new boss man. I'm not sure that I ever saw any of them again, but I have never forgotten them although it has been almost six decades since that day.

They went back to their labors unaware of what a deep and lasting impression their acts of compassion and devotion had made on a frightened, fragile ten-year-old white boy, and perhaps in some mysterious way had helped to set his sails to navigate some rough racial seas some thirty or thirty-five years in the future.

What I remember about my father's funeral is not what the ministers did and said. What I remember is what those farm workers did and said. The only words I remember from my father's

41

funeral, except some of the lines from the hymns, are those words spoken by a black man: "We would like to do that."

For this sermon I have had two texts. One from Genesis, the second chapter: "The Lord God formed Adam of dust from the ground, and breathed into Adam's nostrils the breath of life; and Adam became a living being." And from Galatians, the third chapter: "There is neither Jew nor Greek, there is neither slave nor free, there is neither male nor female; for you are all one in Christ Jesus. And if you are Christ's then you are Abraham's offspring, heirs according to promise."

Philippians 1:3-11

When Remembering
Is More Than Reminiscence

The setting and shape of this sermon are obvious. It was preached at Covenant Presbyterian Church, Tuscaloosa, Alabama, on the occasion of the fortieth anniversary of the founding of that congregation.

The church was officially organized on January 30, 1949. I was the first pastor. I remained pastor until May, 1964.

The sermon itself is mostly a narrative of how I came to accept the call, and the early days of the church's life. I felt that many people in the present congregation knew very little, if anything, about the beginnings of Covenant, and that it would be appropriate for them to learn something of the rock from which they were hewn. The scripture text itself is not dealt with directly until the conclusion of the sermon.

It was December, 1948 — Christmastime. I was a young, skinny preacher barely in my twenties. (I won't say which end of the twenties I was in, but I was in them.) I had already served one pastorate and was fresh from a year at Princeton Seminary where I had received a Th.M. degree. Well, I was not all that "fresh from." I had been unemployed for several months, sponging off my school-teacher mother in a tiny apartment in Marion, Alabama. I had met with search committees and preached in vacant pulpits all over the Southeast, but nothing ever came of it. If I liked them, they didn't like me. If they liked me, I didn't like them. I felt no particular excitement or challenge about any of the places I had visited. I was beginning to wonder about this preaching business, and my part in it.

43

Then one day in December a phone call came. Could I come to Tuscaloosa the next Sunday and preach for a small group of people who were meeting in the Red Cross Auditorium at Northington? They were considering starting a new church.

Well, I had heard of that crowd before. While I was still at Princeton, Mr. Partridge, the Superintendent of Home Missions for old Tuscaloosa Presbytery, had written me about a proposed new work in east Tuscaloosa and wanted to know if I would be interested.

Of course, I wasn't interested. I could not see myself as a pioneer or innovator. I had no intention of starting from scratch. I wanted a real church, a well-established congregation, a beautiful building, preferably paid for, stained-glass windows, a robed choir, a pipe organ, a paneled study with plenty of bookshelves, and a secretary in the next office.

When I got home Mr. Partridge kept pestering me about east Tuscaloosa. Finally in near desperation I drove to Tuscaloosa one day and rode around with Mr. Partridge, C. E. Williams, John Weaver, and Gordon Langford. We saw the little lot which the presbytery had purchased at the corner of Hargrove Road and Prince Avenue. It was ridiculously small. We drove around the neighborhood. I went back to Marion not much impressed.

Now here they came again. They had started to meet and they wanted me to come preach next Sunday. "All right, I'll go and get it over with. After all, I've got nothing else to do next Sunday, and I need the money."

That day was gray, gloomy, and chilly with a drizzle of rain. I had some difficulty finding Northington. Northington was a big, sprawling building all under one roof. It had been a military hospital during World War II. Now it housed the city hospital, an elementary school, student housing for university students, a cafeteria, a cleaning plant, and the Red Cross Auditorium.

One needed a guiding star to find the auditorium through twists and turns and long corridors.

Finally there it was — the most unattractive place for worship I had ever seen. Bare, dim, ugly. Clanging folding metal chairs; a makeshift pulpit. I think there was a crude manger with hay and some canned goods piled in it for the poor. There may have been a pot of red poinsettias, but if so, that was the only touch of beauty in the place. The most striking feature of the room was the stage curtain. It was made like a crazy quilt with all kinds of material in various colors and shapes sewed together. Two masks — comedy and tragedy — leered down at us from the curtain. That was the background before which I was to lead worship.

A little group of about 25 people was almost lost in that big, empty auditorium. They greeted me cordially, and almost immediately I began to experience an "at home" feeling. I conferred with Mrs. C. E. Williams about the hymns, and the service began with Mrs. C. E. Williams playing the somewhat out of tune piano.

I had brought no particular enthusiasm to this service, but as it moved along something began to happen. The singing of Christmas carols filled that bare room with beauty. As I read the familiar Christmas story I began to be aware again of its wonder and joy, and I felt that the people felt it, too. I remember nothing specific about the sermon except that I began to sense a freedom that I had not known in months.

After the service the people and I seemed reluctant to leave. We stood around and talked. They asked me to come back the next Sunday, and without hesitation I said I would. As I drove back to Marion my heart was strangely warmed, and I tried to figure out what had happened that day.

The next Sunday the Red Cross Auditorium was still ugly, but somehow I did not notice it quite so much. I was looking forward to seeing those people again, people whom I already felt were my friends — folk like C. E. and Clara Williams, George and Adalaide Howard, John and Oliver Weaver, George and Catherine Johnson, Bob and Helen Ross, and others whom there is not time to mention.

Again there was that Mysterious Presence, an intangible quality of awe, a feeling of the rightness of things. I agreed to come back for a third Sunday. "What am I doing?" I asked myself. "I had intended to come up here once and that would be it. Why do I keep coming back?"

After the third service the group met, came to me and said, "We want you to come be our preacher."

45

I did not say, "Thank you, but I'm not interested. This just isn't my kind of situation." I did not say, "Well, let me think about it and pray about it. I'll let you know." Rather I said, "Yes, I'll come!"

On my way back to Marion that afternoon I began to think "What have I done? How crazy can you get? Where am I going to live? (Housing was hard to find in Tuscaloosa in 1949.) How am I going to get around? (I did not own a car. I had borrowed my mother's car to make those trips to Tuscaloosa.) What have I got to buy a car with? And what about salary? (Nothing had been said about salary.) And another thing — how long are we going to have to stay at Northington? How can that little group of people ever raise enough money to build a church? And what about that little lot on Prince Avenue? It is not big enough for a church, and where are we going to park?"

But in spite of all the questions and the uncertainties I had no doubts. This was the place for me, as unlikely as it seemed and as unsuited as I seemed for the situation.

What had happened in those three Sundays was that I learned something that I should already have known about what makes a church. It isn't beautiful buildings, stained-glass windows, a pipe organ, a comfortable study, as significant and helpful as all these are. A church can have all this and still be as dull and dead as yesterday's newspaper.

What it takes to make a church is people committed to Jesus Christ, dedicated, enthusiastic, who have a vision and are determined to spend time and energy toward it; who are willing to take risks, to put their faith into practice, and who love each other. That's what I had discovered in that little group at Northington.

But how did they get that way? Not because they were better than anybody else, but because the Spirit of God had gotten hold of them, brought them together, and given them a mission. It was the Holy Spirit at work in, among, and through that group of people — and an even greater miracle is that by contagion the Holy Spirit got hold of me, too, at least for a while.

We thought it would take several months before the congregation was ready officially to form a church, but things moved more rapidly than any of us expected. On the last Sunday in January,

1949, a commission of Tuscaloosa Presbytery met at the Red Cross Auditorium to constitute the congregation into Covenant Presbyterian Church.

It was a cold, stormy day. It had snowed the night before; ice covered the trees and the roads. But in spite of the weather and dangerous driving conditions the auditorium was almost full. We went through the *Book of Church Order* and performed almost every ritual except a wedding, a funeral, and the Lord's Supper. We organized the church; we received 91 charter members, most by letter, some by reaffirmation of faith, some by profession of faith and baptism; we elected, ordained, and installed elders and deacons; and we called and installed a minister. I'm not sure it was legal to do all that in one service, but we did it.

I've thought back on the place where it all began and have concluded that Northington Red Cross Auditorium was not an inappropriate place after all for a church to be born, and that it was surrounded by a good many unorthodox Christian symbols.

It began at Christmastime — the season when we celebrate the birth of Christ. And where was Christ born? Not in a cathedral; not in a palace; not surrounded by beauty. He was born in a place about as bare and dim and uninviting as was that auditorium.

And what about that crazy quilt curtain? What was it made of? It was made of all sorts of different fabrics, colors, shapes, and sizes which came from different places. But all these were sewn together to make a unity. Those pieces sewn together were one; the curtain could do what no one of those pieces could do alone. What better picture of the church — diverse, varied, maybe even some clashing shapes and colors — but all one and working together.

And Comedy and Tragedy — those masks that we tried to cover up on special occasions like Easter and Christmas? Well, isn't the gospel a paradox of comedy and tragedy?

What could be more illogical, even comical, than the way God decided to redeem the world? Couldn't he have set everything right with one fell swoop of majestic power? But he chose to come himself in human flesh and walk among us, to be one of us, to be with us, to share our lot. What a strange role for God.

47

What does comedy do? It makes us laugh; it brings joy; it gives an exhilarating lift to life. Does not the deepest joy in life come from the gospel of Jesus Christ? And, of course, the gospel involves tragedy. It takes evil and suffering, sin and death seriously, and weeps because of them. It takes all these things upon itself and agonizes over them. What is the central Christian symbol? The cross — the symbol of the ultimate tragedy, the symbol of what human evil can do to divine goodness.

But comedy triumphs in the end. The resurrection of Jesus Christ is the epitome of victory and the final assurance of hope.

Now let me recall one more thing. I've talked a good deal about the unprepossessing appearance of the place of Covenant's birth. Well, I wasn't all that much of a promising, prepossessing preacher either. This was brought home to me a few years later.

On the day the church was organized a photographer from the *Tuscaloosa News* was present and took some pictures. These appeared in the paper the next day. One of them was of the group of newly-elected officers — all men in those benighted days. And there I was in the midst of them, skinny, scared, with the expression of a bewildered owl on my face.

For several years after that someone would put these pictures on the bulletin board during the month of January. One day I was standing there looking at them along with Bob Ross. Bob studied the pictures for a while, then said, "When this church started we must have been hard up for a preacher to take you."

And all I could say was, "You were."

Now perhaps all this, especially to the more recent members of this community of faith, has seemed the reminiscence of an old man come back after forty years to talk about the olden days. And to some degree that is true. But the remembering I have been doing is far more than reminiscence. I am trying to remember and to encourage you to remember in the biblical meaning of remembering.

Have you ever thought about what a significant role remembering plays in the history of God's people, both in the Old and the New Testaments? The people of Israel were always being called to remember the mighty acts of God, to remember what God had done for and through them. Remember how God called Abraham and

Sarah to go to a new land, how he made promises to them which included blessings through them for all the nations of the earth. Remember in particular the Exodus when God by a powerful hand led Israel out of bondage in Egypt, across the wilderness for forty years, and into the Promised Land. The prophets were always calling upon Israel to remember the covenant and to remember God's commandments and keep them. And in the New Testament. Remember the words and the works of Jesus. At the empty tomb the angel said to the women, "Remember how he told you while he was still in Galilee ..." And they remembered his words. At the Table of the Lord, "This do in remembrance of me."

Remembering in the biblical sense is not nostalgia; it is not recalling a romantic golden age. It is bringing the past into the present; it is making the past alive again; it is remembering the foundation upon which the future is to be built.

The congregation at Philippi was the apostle Paul's favorite church. He had a more cordial and close relationship with them than with any other congregation he had founded. That is not to say that the Philippian Church was perfect, without problems, tensions, misunderstandings. For it was made up of human beings as are all churches.

Paul maintained an affectionate relationship with them through the years. He revisited them several times. They sent representatives to visit him in prison, and they expressed their concern for him in tangible ways. He wrote letters to them. In the letter to the Philippians which has been preserved Paul talks about remembering and he talks about his confidence for the future.

"I thank my God for every remembrance of you...." One reason he remembered with joy and thanksgiving was because of their participation in the gospel from the beginning until the present. Because of their strong and vital past he could express confidence concerning them for the future. Not so much confidence in them alone as confidence in God who had called them together in the first place and who had been working through them all these years.

"I am sure that he who began a good work in you will bring it to completion at the day of Jesus Christ," he wrote. Paul could not

Mark 14:32-50

Battleground And Victory

This sermon was preached at Covenant Presbyterian Church, Tuscaloosa, Alabama, on Maundy Thursday, 1958.

This was one of the rare occasions when I memorized the sermon and sought to preach it exactly as written. It seems to me that the rhythm, cadence, and sound of the words are important for this particular sermon. The purpose of the sermon is to bring the hearers into the Garden of Gethsemane where they can share to some extent the emotions Jesus must have endured during that night of prayer. The sermon is designed to appeal to the heart more than to the head, and to create an atmosphere of quiet contemplation as the congregation considers the significance of Jesus' suffering and death on our behalf.

Tread softly here, for this is hallowed ground. If you must speak, then whisper only, and in most reverent tones. Stoop not to pluck a careless leaf. Toss no casual stone against the gnarled trunks of the olive trees. But stand, or better kneel, with head bared and bowed. In silence wait. In trembling awe behold this holy ground as if with blood it were baptized, as if upon this sacred soil there lay a host of quiet graves of those who struggled, fought, and died that you might have the costly gift of life and liberty.

They call this place a garden, and so it is. A quiet place with friendly olive trees, the song of birds, soft breezes, and the smell of flowers sweet and bright. But this place is a battleground, for here is fought in desperate conflict the most decisive struggle in human history.

Tread softly here, for you walk in God's Gethsemane. Dare not break the sacred silence, for here one man writhes in agonizing prayer. Three who were told to watch and pray doze into languid slumber. Eight others, beyond the struggle's sight and sound, sit in fear and wonder, while one more has gone into the city to sell his soul at a bargain price.

This is no neutral ground. The battle is for you and me and all humankind. We are caught up, involved, and set upon our destiny by reason of its outcome.

And yet but one man fights the battle. No armies tread this solemn place. No chariots of war leave their ruts along the garden path. He comes. The Man of Sorrows comes to face the lonely wrestling. He does not plunge at once into the solitary conflict, but gradually lets go of human companionship. Surrounded by eleven friends he crosses Kidron's brook. Then he stops.

"Sit here while I go and pray yonder." Eight of them remain. But three of them, Peter, James, and John, follow farther still until by look and word he lets them know that there are steps ahead which he must take alone.

Never had they seen him so distressed and sorrowful. Oh, they had seen him weep, at Lazarus' tomb, for instance, but never so borne down as now. "My soul is very sorrowful, even unto death; remain here, and watch."

Now the battle is joined. The Son of God, the Son of Man, is face to face with mystery and is confronted by the final choice from which there is no turning.

"Abba, Father, all things are possible to you; remove this cup from me."

He is only 33, and no one wants to die at 33. He has seen crosses and watched the crucified hang for days and plead for death. Who is to doubt that he, like anyone, would shrink from this? Is there not some other way? There is still time to turn back, to slip beneath the night's protective shade and return to Galilee to preach and heal and serve. Can there not be some compromise which would serve to give God's message to the world? Must it be now, and must it be death?

Thus boldly before his Father he states his desire and yearning. He does not veil the groping of his soul to find and grasp his

Father's will. To know and accept that will joyfully, that is his struggle and his battleground.

Back from prayer he comes to seek once more the support and understanding of his human friends. It is little that he asks of them: a look, a word, a laying on of hands upon his shoulder.

But the three who love him most, Peter, James, and John, are asleep. How can they sleep? But who am I to ask this question? How often I have refused to share his struggle and have slumbered while the Son of God prays in agony.

His struggle is not a shrinking from a pain no flesh was ever meant to bear, but from the weight of the world's sin upon his spotless soul. He is not pleading for a way out, but for a way into the Father's holy will. The battle is to merge his will with God's own will and to be satisfied with the union.

At last the victory's won. The cup will not pass. The cross still waits. Pain must come and with it death; with the cup a strengthening hand to hold it; with the cross the world's redemption; with the death a victory.

See the victor rise from prayer. Back he comes to his disciples, not now seeking from them comfort and support, but offering to them strength and hope.

"Are you still sleeping and taking your rest? It is enough; the hour has come; the Son of Man is betrayed into the hand of sinners. Rise, let us be going; see, my betrayer is at hand."

Boldly, serenely, he goes out to meet the worst that human sin can do. But the victory is already won. It is won in these words, "Your will be done."

There is nothing of fear and defeat in these words. They are spoken in a tone of holy, perfect trust. It is to his Father whom he speaks. He speaks in surrender, yes; but surrender to an everlasting love, to a love which works only good and redeems the deepest pain.

Tread softly here, for on this sacred ground the cause is won, and God's holy will is victor on this day. The cross, the grave, sin, and death are vanquished in defeat.

It is enough. The hour has come. Rise, let us be going, for this is victory day.

Templates And Story-Sermons

The buttonholer on my sewing machine uses templates. If I need a five-eighths-inch buttonhole, I put in the five-eighths-inch template. If I need a one-inch buttonhole, I use the one-inch template. The template's control over the shape of the buttonhole is secondary, derivative. I first select the template based on the garment I am sewing and the size of the button I want to use.

Of course, it is possible that I might lose all my templates but one. Then I would be obliged to put the same size buttonhole on a doll dress as on a heavy winter coat. Similarly some beginning preachers seem to have only a single template. Sometimes in my role as teacher of preaching, I find myself encouraging students to use the one template again and again until it becomes a familiar tool, ready at hand. My reasoning is that one pattern, deeply felt and thoroughly understood, sometimes can provide a secure basis from which the beginning preacher can experiment with variations and new patterns.

I imagine that most of us preachers end up with a few templates that are our favorites or that produce our most effective sermons. These templates are part of what constitutes our "unique style" or "voice." My intent here is not to reduce Ormond's sermons to four paint-by-number patterns. But rather I want to suggest that with these four patterns as part of his homiletical psyche, Ormond is able to compose poignant and provocative sermons again and again. These are templates that most preachers, with practice, can claim for their own, adapt to fit their own idiosyncrasies, and add to their stockroom, quiver, work apron, or drawer of available sermon forms.

One template of sermons is the story-sermon,[4] and Ormond is an excellent storyteller. The seven sermons I will examine here are "Why Can't We Call Him Clarence?" "Oh, No; Not Again ...,"

"The Cross Of Barabbas," "A Lamb For A Household," "A Sermon In Clay," "When Remembering Is More Than Reminiscence," and "Battleground And Victory." I do not plan to analyze each in detail but only to make some comparisons and draw some contrasts. There is a template called story-sermon; and there are numerous variations of which these sermons are fine examples.

Let me begin with some very obvious observations. "Why Can't We Call Him Clarence?" is pure story; it is unusual in that it unfolds entirely through dialogue. "The Cross Of Barabbas" and "A Lamb For A Household" also are pure story, told from a first-person point of view. In each of these sermons, Ormond has created two characters whose dialogue or implied dialogue constitutes the narrative. In each of these sermons one of the characters in the course of the sermon fairly explicitly states the meaning or meanings that Ormond has derived from his study of the specified biblical passage. "Oh, No; Not Again ..." is more directly a retelling of a biblical story. At the end of this sermon Ormond steps out of the story and reflects briefly on its meaning for "us" and "our faithfulness." Long labels these two related patterns "A single story" and "Story/reflection" (Long 1989, p. 129).

"A Sermon In Clay" and "When Remembering Is More Than Reminiscence" are different from the four story-sermons discussed above in that they retell personal stories from Ormond's life. Yet structurally "A Sermon In Clay" is pure story, or "a single story," and "When Remembering Is More Than Reminiscence" is story followed by reflection on a number of meanings for the present congregation, or "story/reflection." These second two sermons differ from the first four also because they intentionally invite multiple interpretations, in contrast to the specific range of meanings that is spelled out by one of the characters or by the preacher in each of the first four sermons. "A Sermon In Clay," like a finely crafted short story, leaves the congregation to arrive at its own meanings. Ormond merely suggests theological connections by framing the story between two biblical passages. In contrast, "When Remembering Is More Than Reminiscence" offers a smorgasbord of possible meanings from which the members of the congregation can choose — what it takes to make a church, the appropriateness of a patchwork quilt curtain, the gospel as comedy and tragedy, the role of remembering among the people of God, confidence in the future.

"Battleground And Victory," also pure story, is unique in that the congregation functions as characters in the story. From the opening words of the sermon, Ormond cautions the congregation to "tread softly." Later he directs their gaze to "see the victor rise from prayer." And at the end, he leaves them to draw their own conclusions. As he writes in his preface to this sermon, "the sermon is designed ... to create an atmosphere of quiet contemplation as the congregation considers the significance of Jesus' suffering and death on our behalf." Anticipating the discussion below about inductive and deductive preaching, I would classify all seven of these sermons as inductive; they allow meaning to emerge during the course of the storytelling. What happens, when a worshiper's or a reader's imagination is engaged by the imagination of the preacher, is that personal meanings emerge tailored to the life of the worshiper or reader. I will relate two examples. As I was rereading "Why Can't We Call Him Clarence?" I began thinking prayerfully about my own child, now five years old, who was born when I was 42. I felt a keen affinity for Betty, while at the same time I found myself on a roller coaster ride of personal thoughts and feelings about my and my daughter's futures. "Oh, No; Not Again ..." sparked a response that made me pause and jot down a note to myself. Near the end of the sermon Ormond quotes from the conclusion of the biblical version of the story:

> And the Lord said, "Hear what the unrighteous judge says. And will not the Lord grant justice to his chosen ones, who cry to him day and night? Will he delay long in helping them? I tell you, he will quickly grant justice to them."

Having read those words, I wrote this note to myself: "Pray for justice. I pray for places, not injustices." The sermon inspired me to rethink my prayer list, to lift my voice with those who cry for justice, to add to my prayers for South Africa and Haiti and Bosnia prayers for those oppressed by unjust power structures, by greed, by indifference and neglect. Neither of these personal responses is outside the range of significations suggested by the sermons. The power for me of these personal responses, however, is that they are my own conclusions, they are the whispers of the Holy Spirit in my ear and heart, they are particular prods along my life journey toward sanctification, they are the ways God once again calls me by name to a life of faith and trust.

Effective story-preaching, and particularly inductive story-preaching like this, depends on the ability of the preacher's imagination to awaken responses in the worshipers' imaginations. Four characteristics of Ormond's storytelling are noteworthy, for they lend evocative power to his narratives and are especially valuable in his story-sermons. The examples here are taken from "A Sermon In Clay," although other examples could be found elsewhere.

First, there is Ormond's capacity for vivid detail: as reader or worshiper, I smell "the cloying sweetness of florist flowers"; I watch the cloud of dust "at first no bigger than a person's hand" as it snakes "its way around the little general store"; I see the "dusty faces streaked with tears." With a carefully chosen sensory word, Ormond re-creates the moment so that it lives again in his own, in my, and in others' imaginations.

Second, Ormond's emotions are no strangers to his sermons. At times he laughs easily and lovingly at himself and at the foibles of a seminary community. At other times he betrays a winsome vulnerability and an openness to emotions too often in the church kept in check. In "A Sermon In Clay" he does not shrink from "the deep, hollow hurt within me." Consequently, this sermon taps the imaginations of the worshipers for their own memories of "fear, uncertainty — and even embarrassment."

Third, Ormond's images, though sparing, are striking because they combine sensual vividness and emotional depth. There are several such images in "A Sermon In Clay." For example, Ormond describes his uncle and aunt as enfolding him and his mother "into their family as if we were quivering birds with broken wings," and he speaks of the unfilled grave as a "deep wound in the earth."

Finally, Ormond occasionally uses alliteration so that sound reinforces content in the hearts and minds of his congregation. In "A Sermon In Clay" I repeatedly find one particular combination of image and alliteration moving. Referring to the change that is imminent in his life, Ormond says, "It was as if someone had taken an exquisite cut glass bowl and dropped it on a stone floor where it exploded into a multitude of sharp, shining shards." For me, the repeated *sh's* mimic the smooth slicing of a glass fragment and reinforce the idea that this ten-year-old boy's world now holds the potential for cutting again and again and that the boy himself is deeply wounded. A second example of alliteration describes the mound of clay beside the grave as "red, raw, and real." When I say these three words, my mouth pauses ever so slightly to shape the initial *r*. That pause tinges this alliteration with faint self-consciousness, as though the words themselves were demanding that I look at the mound of clay and notice its redness, feel its rawness, and accept its reality.

These four characteristics of Ormond's storytelling are vehicles by which his imagination weaves its spell with words and awakens the imaginations of the worshipers. His touch is deft; his use of techniques spare. At his fingertips are sights, smells, humor, memories, and words. These are the raw materials which he combines to bring each scene to life in the minds and hearts of the congregation.

How does one learn to tell stories? I learned by reading stories and more stories and more stories; and along the way, to my horror, a professor suggested that I try my hand at telling one of my own. How does one learn to tell story-sermons? I learned by reading good story-sermons and by listening to Will Ormond preach his; I pondered what I had learned about storytelling; and one day, when none of my templates would work on a mass of sermon material on my desk, my first story-sermon began to write itself.

Deductive And
Inductive Sermons

This Above All

It you celebrated your fortieth birthday — or younger — in 1995, the term "Lucy Riots" probably means nothing to you. You might also be rather vague about what momentous decision the Supreme Court of the United States handed down in 1954.

But for those of us who were living in Tuscaloosa, Alabama, in 1956, both these events had a tremendous impact on our lives as individuals and as a community.

If you are forty or younger you may find it difficult to believe that prior to 1954 it was against the law in Alabama, and in most Southern states, for white people and black people to attend the same schools. This included state-supported universities and colleges. In 1954 the Supreme Court handed down a decision which declared that such segregation of public schools was unconstitutional. In spite of this ruling, many institutions, including the University of Alabama, resisted the enrollment of black students.

In 1956 the University was under court order to admit its first black student. Her name was Authurine Lucy. When she was finally admitted, riots broke out in the city of Tuscaloosa and on the campus. The atmosphere was extremely tense, not only in the city and on the campus, but also in the church. The violence increased. These riots became known as the "Lucy Riots."

This sermon was preached in Covenant Presbyterian Church, Tuscaloosa, the Sunday following the Lucy Riots. It seeks to deal with a serious crisis in the community by the use of Romans, the thirteenth chapter, and is an example of how scripture can be used to address a specific situation in the community.

(This sermon reflects the historical era when it was prepared and preached. This was before there was much concern for inclusive language. Therefore, I have left the language as it was at the time.)

Today is Race Relations Sunday. It has been so designated by the National Council of Churches. It is so marked by our own denomination. Never since its first observance 34 years ago has it been so strategically timed, at least insofar as our own community is concerned.

Doubtless there are those who feel that in the present charged atmosphere in which we live the less said about race the better. Perhaps some of you had hoped for this one hour of quiet and calm in the House of God to be spared any mention of the turbulence which has engulfed us.

If I were free to follow my natural bent of the avoidance of controversy and the pursuit of peace at any price, I would ignore the subject. But I am not free. I am a bond slave of Jesus Christ; therefore, I am bound insofar as I can discern his Spirit's leading to follow his will and not my own.

I do not see how I can be true to my calling, true to my Church, true to the community, and most especially, true to him whom I profess to serve unless I seek, however inadequately and feebly, to bring to bear upon the tensions of our time some light from the Word of God. And it must be from the Word of God, for who among us is sufficient for these things? Who among us is wise enough or prophetic enough to untangle the complex web of conflicting forces in which we are caught?

It seems to me that Romans, the thirteenth chapter, has some clear and definite things to say to us in our present crisis.

One of the questions which has erupted suddenly in our midst and turned the eyes of the whole world upon us is this: Where is the final authority? What forces shall be obeyed? What powers shall prevail?

Is the final authority the government of the nation of which we are citizens, or is it the enforced will of a group of self-appointed defenders of the status quo? Shall we obey the law of the land, or shall we obey the threatening decrees of an undisciplined mob? Shall the powers of decency, order, and reasonableness prevail, or shall the forces of prejudice, hate, and violence win the day?

Paul, writing in the thirteenth chapter of Romans, seems to make the Christian's position abundantly clear. He writes, "Let every person be subject to the governing authorities. For there is no authority except from God, and those that exist have been instituted by God. Therefore he who resists the authorities resists what God has appointed, and those who resist will incur judgment" (Romans 13:1-2).

This would seem to be so plain as to need little comment. It is the Christian's duty to obey the law and uphold orderly government. God has ordained an organized society for the welfare of mankind, to encourage good conduct, and to judge wickedness. Those who set themselves against law and order and who seek by violence and force to nullify the law are setting themselves against God's order and are placing themselves under his judgment. The University of Alabama was seeking to obey the law quietly and calmly when forces of violence and hate stepped in to try to nullify the law. Let those who take part in or condone this breach of the peace remember that law and order are ordained of God.

But if it is un-Christian to flaunt the law by violent means, is it not the Christian's duty to obey the law by peaceful means? Much time and thought, energy and discussion have been expended in our country to find ways to circumvent the law as expressed in the much maligned decision of the Supreme Court. Recognizing that this decision has confronted us with problems which seem almost insurmountable and which are so complex and deep-seated as to take years to solve, ought it not be the Christian's attitude to give our best thought and effort and energy to seeking calm and workable ways to obey the law rather than exhausting ourselves in trying to nullify the law? Granted that when those who are supported in their efforts by the law flaunt their gains in our faces and parade their triumphs, it makes the situation tremendously more difficult. But that does not excuse us as Christians from our responsibility as citizens to obey the law and to seek to solve our problems within the framework of organized, orderly government.

But Christians are citizens of two realms and are under a higher law than that of the state. Christians are citizens of their particular nations, but they are citizens also of the Kingdom of God. They owe allegiance to the laws of the land, but they have a higher loyalty to the royal law of God.

65

Paul recognizes this dual citizenship, for he follows his discussion of the Christian's duty as a citizen in the secular realm with a brief summary of the law which must govern the Christian in every area of life: "Owe no man anything, except to love one another; for he who loves his neighbor has fulfilled the law. The commandments ... are summed up in this sentence, 'You shall love your neighbor as yourself.' Love does no wrong to a neighbor; therefore love is the fulfilling of the law" (Romans 13:8-10).

Our present crisis and the social revolution of which it is a symptom will not be resolved by legislation, litigation, court decisions, or the due processes of law. Since the crisis has to do with the relation of people one to another, then the determining factor will be the human element of attitude, feelings, emotions, humility, and willingness to get along with one another. Only within the framework of Christian love can we have the grace to work out our differences. Christian love is not determined by the lovableness of the other person nor is it conditioned by whether or not there is a mutual and equal response of love. It is a gift of God, a ruling principle that involves goodwill, forgiveness, and humility. It is our response to God's love for us in giving himself to us, and it reaches out to all men everywhere.

Since we as Christians are under the law of love, it is our duty not to do or say anything that will add to or encourage the atmosphere of hate and prejudice which is all too evident in our community. It is also our Christian part to do any positive acts which will demonstrate our love for all people. For the law of love is an active force, and it must find ways of expression in other ways than simply refraining from evil.

In the last part of the thirteenth chapter of Romans, Paul reminds us of the urgency which attends the Christian life. He says that the Christian is living in a new day, and that there is only one source of power for living a Christian life under any circumstances.

There is time only to touch on these points. Paul speaks with urgency about the time being pressing. It is time to rouse ourselves. Christians cannot put off forever the facing of issues and trying to solve problems and find answers. The Christian life is a growth, a pilgrimage, a moving on to new insights and new advantages in faith.

The Christian lives in the light of a newly dawning day. His eyes must be toward the future, not always straining toward the past. He must put on the armor of light in order to live in the new day. And this above all — put on the Lord Jesus Christ.

We are Christians only by God's grace. When I surrender to him so that he takes over my life, then it is not I who live, but Christ who lives in me.

Surely we who are Christians believe that in the gospel of Christ there is the answer to the complexities of our problems of race. The events of the past week have thrust upon us the necessity of searching more diligently for those answers.

If the answers are in Christ, then why have we not found them before now? I can think of only two reasons. Either we do not know Christ well enough, or we do see the answer in him, but we choose to be blind. Having eyes we deliberately see not; having ears we hear not.

If either of these conditions is true, or if a mixture of these two is nearer to the facts, then two courses are open to us.

First, to re-examine this gospel with open and humble hearts and without preconceived notions; to seek to know Christ more intimately than we know our closest relative or friend; to surrender to his leading, no matter what the cost.

The other course is to pray in agonizing repentance for forgiveness; to ask God to open our eyes and unstop our ears, and to give us the courage and the wisdom to follow what we see and hear. Neither course, nor a combination of them, is easy. Being a Christian was never meant to be easy. But when the Lord made the way straight and narrow he never meant for us to walk it without him.

Acts 28:17, 30-31

Thank God And Take Courage

This sermon is historically conditioned in two ways. It was delivered on the Sunday before Thanksgiving, 1983. It seeks to put the motif of thanksgiving into the context of the national and world situation of the time.

It also recalls another Thanksgiving season twenty years before when the nation had been plunged into mourning by the assassination of President Kennedy.

The purpose of the sermon is to encourage Christians to be grateful to God at all times, especially in times when a feeling of gratitude may be difficult to express.

While the circumstances recounted for 1983 may not fit later periods in our history, it is safe to say that during almost any Thanksgiving season there are likely to be enough distressing situations in the world to make a sermon such as this appropriate.

It is not always easy to remember where one was or what one was doing on a particular day twenty years ago. But if you are thirty years or older, then I am sure that most of you remember where you were and what you were doing on the afternoon of November 22, 1963, twenty years ago this Tuesday.

I was helping a friend move into a new house. We had a little portable radio playing on an empty shelf. Suddenly the program was interrupted. President Kennedy had been shot in Dallas, Texas. We stopped and listened in stunned silence. The extent of his injuries was not known at the moment. Hope revived a little.

"Maybe it is not so bad. It can't be; it simply can't be."

But soon the ominous announcement came. The president was dead. An assassin's bullet had shattered his brain.

The horror, the grief, the senselessness of it all swept over us. My friend and I abandoned our work and returned to our homes, depressed, sickened, confused, bewildered.

After I had had a little while to try to get things back in focus it dawned on me — "Sunday is the Sunday before Thanksgiving."

I was the full-time pastor of a church in Alabama in 1963, and on Sunday I had planned to read the Presidential Thanksgiving Proclamation and preach a Thanksgiving sermon.

Suddenly it all seemed terribly ironic. The President who had called the nation to thanksgiving was now dead, and the nation was plunged into mourning. My Thanksgiving sermon seemed shallow and superficial. What could I say? How could I change the sermon so that it made any kind of sense in circumstances such as this? Wouldn't it be better simply to cancel Thanksgiving and give way to grief, despair, and uncertainty?

I must admit that I do not remember what I did with that Thanksgiving sermon, but we did not cancel Thanksgiving that year.

Now Thanksgiving is upon us again. What is our national mood this time? Perhaps we would not all agree on the answer to that question, but is it a mood of settled tranquility, of calm certainty, of assured peace, of happy unity, with a warm feeling of well-being?

It does not seem so. Ours is a time when a passenger jet with 269 people can be shot out of the sky; when almost 250 of our young Marines are blown to bits while they watch a fratricidal war which seems to have no solution. Superpowers move their nuclear missiles about the face of the earth like grotesque chess pieces. They face each other like two people standing waist deep in gasoline, arguing about parity in firepower because one has twelve matches and the other has only ten.

By this time some of you are probably thinking, "What a gloomy way to begin a Thanksgiving sermon." I agree. But perhaps it is not an entirely incongruous way.

For it may be that against such a somber background Thanksgiving can avoid the danger of shallowness and superficiality. Perhaps it is in times which do not naturally generate a welling up of thankful feeling that we need to seek to recapture a sense of genuine gratitude.

For the Christian attitude of thanksgiving does not depend on circumstances which are always favorable, nor is it based upon a series of uninterrupted victories and increasing triumphs.

The Christian faith is based on and motivated by thankfulness. Our faith and our ethic are grateful responses to God's deed on our behalf. And at the heart of God's deed for us is a cross — the dark clouds of Calvary, the sun blotted out at noonday, the tragic death of One who did not deserve to die.

If we believe that Jesus' death is for us, that the blood shed on the cross cleanses our sin, that his death conquers death, then we live out of gratitude — not to pay a debt we cannot pay, nor to earn a gift we do not deserve, but to express to God our thanks for his inexpressible gift. Therefore, Thanksgiving is not a uniquely American secular holiday. Genuine thanksgiving is deeply theological and characteristically Christian.

If this is true, then we would expect to find in the New Testament evidence of those who recognized the reality of life in this world, but who could give thanks to God in spite of it. There also must be examples of how Christians can, without consciously thinking about it, become sources of thanksgiving and courage for others.

Both such examples are evident in the experience of the apostle Paul. Paul's life was characterized by relentless travel, illness, conflict with those outside the church who had been his colleagues, and conflict within the church with fellow Christians. He endured shipwreck, beatings, stoning, and imprisonment. And yet he was forever thanking God.

A good example is his Letter to the Philippians. He wrote this letter while he was in a Roman prison facing an uncertain future, not knowing whether he would be set free or executed. But the letter literally pulsates with joy. A characteristic line in the letter is the exhortation: "Have no anxiety about anything, but in everything in prayer and supplication with thanksgiving let your requests be made known to God. And the peace of God, which passes all understanding, will keep your hearts and minds in Christ Jesus" (Philippians 4:6-7).

But Paul also had his times of depression and despair. For example, in one of his letters to the Corinthians he could speak of

71

being "so utterly, unbearably crushed that we despaired of life itself" (2 Corinthians 1:8).

But it is on his voyage to Rome, so vividly described by Luke in the last two chapters of Acts, that we see the Paul who lived gratefully and confidently through danger and disaster, and also the Paul who himself received from others that which made him thank God and take courage.

Paul is on his way to Rome by sea to appear before the highest court in the land, the court of Caesar. On the way the ship encounters a violent storm which threatens the very lives of all on board. But through it all Paul is the calm, confident one, giving directions and advice, encouraging the others to eat in the midst of the storm, assuring them that none of them will be lost.

They are shipwrecked on the island of Malta. After being marooned for three months they finally take ship and make their way toward Rome. They land on the coast of Italy and begin the last lap of their journey on foot, going along the famed Appian Way.

One can imagine Paul's thoughts as he draws nearer to the city. It has been a long, difficult voyage. Thus far he has kept up his spirits and the spirits of those who travel with him. But could it be that now near the end of the journey even the spirits of the great apostle Paul should begin to falter?

What awaits him? How will his fellow Jews receive him? He has been received with hostility by them in many other places. He had written a long letter to the Christian community in Rome, but most of them did not know him by sight. What rumors might they have heard about him? Would they be suspicious of him, coming to Rome in chains? And what of Caesar? Who could predict about Caesar? How long would it be before his case was heard? Would the verdict be freedom or death?

Step by step Rome draws nearer. Paul and his companions pass by the many elaborate burial monuments which line the Appian Way. The great city with its multitude of uncertainties looms ahead.

But then something happens which makes all the difference. It is nothing spectacular. No blinding light, no voice from heaven such as Paul saw and heard on the road to Damascus. What happens is so simple as to be hardly worth recording. Or is it so significant that it must be told?

Some of the Christians in Rome hear that Paul is on his way, and they go out to meet him on the road. This is how Luke tells it: "And so we came to Rome. And the brethren there, when they heard of us, came as far as the Forum of Appius and the Three Taverns to meet us. On seeing them Paul thanked God and took courage" (Acts 28:14b-15).

We can almost feel the relief in Paul's soul, the uplift of his spirit, the thankfulness of his heart. Paul did not have to wait to hear their greeting or their message. Their very coming conveyed their concern, their caring, their acceptance of him. They cared enough to come.

Their coming could not assure that the Jews would not be hostile. Their coming would have no effect on Caesar's court or on the verdict pronounced. But still, "on seeing them Paul thanked God and took courage." This simple scene leads me to express deep thanks against the background of somber anxiety at the beginning of Thanksgiving week, 1983.

Thank God for the Church of Jesus Christ. For it is in the church that we can see others coming to meet us, and therefore thank God and take courage. And it is as a part of the church that we can be those who, hearing of others on the uncertain road, can go out to meet them with care, concern, and acceptance. And when they see us, they can thank God and take courage.

Thank God most of all for Jesus Christ himself. For he hears about us human beings floundering in this world on the road to an uncertain future. And he comes out to meet us. His coming is no casual coming, no pleasant stroll while the dew is still on the roses. His coming in care, concern, and acceptance cost him his life. He knows not only where we have been, but he knows where we are going, for he is already there.

Jesus Christ knows we are on the road, and he comes out to meet us. Therefore, we can thank God and take courage.

Foundations

It may be difficult for persons who did not live in the South in the 1960s to comprehend that many "white" congregations had duly approved policies which excluded African-Americans from attending worship. It was a highly emotional issue. It was an expression of segregation at its worst.

Stillman College is a Presbyterian institution in Tuscaloosa, Alabama, with a predominantly black student body. Stillman was founded in 1876 by Southern Presbyterians. Covenant Presbyterian Church from its founding in 1949 had a close and friendly relationship with Stillman.

During the 1960s the students at Stillman began to become active in the civil rights movement. One expression of that activity was to appear at "white" churches and seek to enter for worship. Invariably they were turned away at the front door. None appeared at Covenant.

But much to my dismay and shock, the session, under fear that one might appear some Sunday morning, passed, by a narrow margin, a "closed door policy." This action caused much distress to me as pastor and to many in the congregation. However, we lived with this policy for several months. During that time no black person sought to attend worship. Finally, by another narrow margin, the session reversed the policy.

This sermon was prepared with all the background of the debate in mind. However, I did not know that on the very day it was delivered some students and a black faculty family from Stillman would attend Sunday school and the morning worship service. Their presence made the points of the sermon extremely relevant.

(This sermon is published in *The Unsilent South: Prophetic Preaching in Racial Crisis*, edited by Donald A. Shriver, Jr., John Knox

Press, 1965. A more extensive description of the situation appears in the book.)

———————————

We are met today as a congregation of the Presbyterian Church in the United States. We are members of a denomination committed to certain doctrines and principles. Presbyterians believe that the growth, the effectiveness, and the health of the church depend in large measure upon how well we understand and how surely we live up to these doctrines.

The doctrines of our church are not exclusively Presbyterian, but each one is emphasized and stressed in our creed. From time to time we need to consider the foundations of that creed. I would call your attention to three of those foundations, the three primary ones.

The first of these is the Lordship of Christ. The very earliest Christian creed was "Jesus Christ is Lord," and all the rest of theology is commentary on that brief declaration. Paul wrote, "No one can say 'Jesus is Lord' except by the Holy Spirit." For one to recognize the Lordship of Jesus Christ takes an act of God in the heart of a person.

What do we mean when we say that Jesus is Lord? We mean that he rules, that he is over all, that he directs, that he is sovereign, that to him belong our highest loyalty and allegiance.

Why is he Lord? He is Lord because of who he is in his person. Jesus Christ is one with us; he is human as we are human; he has identified himself with us and understands us from within our humanity. But the very miracle of his humanness is the fact that he is the Word made flesh. Perhaps it is easy for us to picture Jesus in long flowing robes walking along the picturesque lanes of Galilee as he pats little children on the head and speaks gently of peace and love.

But it is not quite so easy to see him as the first chapter of Revelation portrays him — a dazzling figure with eyes like flames of fire, feet like burnished bronze, his voice like the sound of many waters, a sharp two-edge sword issuing from his mouth, and in his hand seven stars symbolizing the universal church. It is difficult for us to grasp those passages of Scripture which say of him, "he is the image of the invisible God"; "in him all things were created"; "he is before all things, and in him all things hold together"; "in him all the fullness of God was pleased to dwell" (Colossians 1:15-17, 19).

This Jesus Christ is not one who is so much like us that we can transfer our feelings, prejudices, and notions to our own image of him. We like to feel that because we think in such and such a manner, Jesus, our human friend, feels exactly the same way about it. No, this one who has revealed himself in human flesh is the Lord of heaven and earth. Before him we bow in awe, worship, and submission. We do not say to him, "Jesus, my dear friend, I would that you would do for me whatsoever I desire." Rather it is for us to fall down before the blinding light of his majesty and cry, "Lord, what would you have me to do?"

Jesus Christ is Lord, also, because of what he has done. He emptied himself, he did not count equality with God a thing to be grasped. But he took upon himself the form of a servant. He suffered unto death. He purchased the church with his own blood, that is, with the complete giving of his life. He did not purchase the church with a few hours of his time after he had taken care of all his own interests. He did not purchase the church with the giving of some of the surplus of his means. He purchased the church with his own blood. Therefore, the church is his, and he is head of it.

We are easily prone to speak of "my church" or "our church" and to assert our proprietorship over it because of what we have given to it or because of some inherited connection with it. But none of us has the right to call the church "mine" except the one who purchased it with his own blood. God himself recognized Jesus' giving of his life, for he raised him from the dead, and gave him all authority and all power and made him the head of the church.

Now what does this Lordship of Christ mean for the church? It means that the church is responsible first of all to Christ. It means that the church makes its decisions not by what it believes to be the desire of the majority of its members nor by the prevailing atmosphere and custom of the time. It means that the officers and members ask about every action, "Is this action being taken under conscious submission to the Lordship of Christ and solely in accordance with his will?"

This question is not an easy one to answer. It almost always involves struggle and the surrender of some of our own cherished desires and preferences. This may sound un-American, but the church is not a democracy. The gospel is not decided by majority vote. The church is a theocracy. It is totalitarian in its rulership. For Christ is its sovereign; he is its absolute authority. Only insofar as the church is ruled by Jesus Christ, its head, is it truly the church. He rules in the church insofar as the congregation in its corporate life and the individual members in their daily relationships submit to the Lordship of Christ.

It is an easy thing to say that we recognize his Lordship, but it is not an easy thing to live by. Far too often we get around it in some such fashion as this: "I am a Christian. I have accepted Christ as my personal Lord and Savior. I am an officer in the church. Therefore, what I think is right is his will. What makes me feel good is Christian. What goes against the grain and disturbs me is wrong."

But this is not surrender to Christ; this is calling upon Christ to surrender to us. To submit to the Lordship of Christ calls for struggle and prayer and the agonizing releasing of our own wills to the will of God. Even Jesus himself had to go through the ordeal of the Garden of Gethsemane as he searched for the will of his Father and sought to bring his own will into conformity with the will of God. If this is the path our Lord had to take, should we hope for a painless and effortless molding of our stubborn wills to the will of God?

But how are we to know the will of the Lord? This leads us to the second foundation, and that is the authority of Scripture.

Christians are the people of the Book. We believe that the Holy Spirit inspired men of old to write the Scriptures and that through them he spoke. But we also believe that the Holy Spirit is eternal and active, and therefore God can and does still speak through these same documents which he caused to be written so long ago. The very first chapter of the Westminster Confession of Faith is "Of the

Holy Scripture." The first question put to church officers upon ordination is, "Do you believe the Scriptures of the Old and New Testaments to be the Word of God, the only infallible rule of faith and practice?" When a person answers that question in the affirmative it means that one accepts the Scriptures as one's guide and authority. It means that where the Scriptures speak one will listen, one will obey, one will act. It means one will always be open for new light to break from the Word of God. It means that one will not be guided by one's own opinion, preferences, nor by the pressures of circumstances, traditions, or groups, but only by the Word of God. Many times we piously state that we follow our conscience in the decisions we make, but conscience is a poor guide unless we can say as did Martin Luther, "My conscience is captive to the Word of God."

If we are to recognize the authority of Scripture and take the Word of God as our guide, then it follows that we must know what that Word is. We must not be content with a causal reading of a verse here and there, but we must come to that Word diligently with open minds and hearts, asking God to speak to us through it. We must not come with minds already made up as to what the Word ought to say or what we would like for it to say. Rather we must come ready to hear what it does say whether we like it or not. Too often we search the Scriptures searching for props for our prejudices. Too often we force the Word to speak our words, rather than letting it, under the Holy Spirit's power, speak God's Word.

It is a dangerous thing to discover what the Word of God really says. For once we have discovered it, we are under obligation, both by reason of our relationship with Christ and the vows we have taken as Christ's disciples, to obey that Word.

The Lordship of Christ and the authority of Scripture lead us to the third foundation, and that is the unity of the Church.

If Jesus Christ is Lord, then he is the head of the church, and the church can have only one head. If the church has one head, then it is one body, and all members are united one to the other. If we are members of his body, then, whether we like it or not, we are united inevitably to all other members of that body. We are united to our fellow Christians whoever and wherever they are, not because we all look alike, not because we all think the same thoughts, not because we are naturally congenial with each other, not because we all have the same background and culture. We are united to our fellow Christians solely because all of us are united to Christ, the head of the church.

The authority of Scripture also leads us to the unity of the church. What is the Bible all about? It is the record of God's mighty acts. It is the record of what God has been doing all through history. And what has he been doing? God has been calling to himself a people, a people for his purpose. This is what he was doing when he called Abraham, when he called Israel, and this is what he is doing now as he calls us, his church, to be the instrument of his purpose in the world. He is calling us to be the instrument of his purpose of reconciliation in this divided world. He is calling his church to demonstrate in its own corporate life that unity which comes from being reconciled to God and to one another.

Our Presbyterian constitution defines the visible church as consisting of "all those who make profession of their faith in the Lord Jesus Christ, together with their children." The church is a colony of heaven set in a pagan world. It is not an earthly club for spiritual aristocrats.

If we are members of the Presbyterian Church in Tuscaloosa, or Eutaw, or Selma, or Linden, then we are members of the whole Presbyterian Church in the United States, then we are members of the church universal. We cannot put restrictions or limitations of our own choosing upon our membership, for we are members one of another.

The Lordship of Christ, the authority of Scripture, and the unity of the church — these are the foundations of Presbyterian doctrine and policy. May we take our stand upon these foundations and never forsake them.

Luke 18:31-43

The Celestial Stop Sign

This sermon was prepared for a regular chapel service at Columbia Seminary.

It begins with a fanciful, imaginary story which centers around the image of a stoplight which interrupts a Presidential motorcade. The hearers soon realize the story is ridiculous. And that is its point.

To many of the people traveling with Jesus on his last visit to Jerusalem the blind beggar by the roadside who called out to him must have seemed equally ridiculous. But Jesus stops, although he is on the most important journey of his life. In fact, the stopping is actually a vital part of that journey. It symbolizes what the journey is about.

In a few sentences the conclusion seeks to challenge the hearers to ask themselves if they would stop in a similar situation.

Can you imagine something like this ever happening?

The President of the United States is scheduled to address the United Nations on an extremely crucial issue of worldwide significance. The very peace of the world may well hang in the balance. The heads of all the nations of the earth are gathered waiting the President's arrival. The exact time has been carefully determined. The route the Presidential procession will follow has been meticulously laid out. All side streets have been blocked so that no cross traffic can interrupt the motorcade.

The long sleek limousines with flags fluttering on their forward fenders are lined up along with motorcade escorts ahead and behind. Secret Service personnel are all in their proper places. The driver of the Presidential automobile has been given precise instructions as to how fast to drive so that the motorcade will arrive at the United Nations building on the split second of the expected time.

The procession begins to move exactly on time. It gathers speed and proceeds at the proper pace. The crowds along the way cheer and wave. The President smiles and acknowledges the cheers.

Then there is a sudden squealing of tires as the driver of the Presidential car slams on the brakes and brings the whole thing to a screeching halt. Consternation reigns among the motorcycle escorts and Secret Service. The President picks himself up off the floor of the back seat. He demands of the driver in language unsuitable for repetition in the pulpit: "Why in the name of common sense have we stopped?"

The driver calmly replies, "We have stopped, Mr. President, because the traffic light suddenly changed from green to red, and now I think it is stuck on red."

The whole world waits. And one overly cautious driver of the Presidential limousine stops for a stupid, insignificant traffic light which is on this day of all days supposed to be ignored.

"Behold. We are going up to Jerusalem, and everything that is written of the Son of Man by the prophets will be accomplished."

Thus did Jesus solemnly speak to his disciples as they were on the road. According to Luke's chronology, Jesus and the disciples have been on the road from Galilee for quite some time. By determined and unrelenting steps Jesus has been moving along, going up to Jerusalem where he has a rendezvous with an incredibly significant destiny. At the end of the road everything written about him by the prophets will be accomplished or fulfilled.

Mounting anticipation and excitement grip those who are traveling with him. They know this is a journey of destiny. They are confused and puzzled by the things Jesus tells them will happen when they get there. What is this talk about the Son of Man being killed and being raised on the third day? They cannot comprehend such talk, but they know that things are moving toward a climax. Jesus has often spoken of the Kingdom of God. Perhaps that is what this journey is all about. Maybe this is a coronation procession. As they draw nearer to the city some of them are convinced of it. When they get to Jerusalem the Kingdom of God will surely come immediately.

Therefore, let the procession move on unhindered. Place no obstacle in the way. And above all, let there be no intrusive, interruptive stop sign in the way — and if there is one, ignore it.

But from somewhere on the edge of the crowd there is a cry, "Son of David, have mercy on me."

There he is — a blind beggar sitting by the road. Clouds of dust from many moving feet billow around him. He has draped his mantle over his head to shield his sightless eyes from the grit of the road.

He is as insignificant and incongruous as a stop sign in the middle of a Presidential procession. Many in the crowd recognize how disruptive is his presence at this time and place, how annoying, how disturbing is his cry.

They seek to silence him. "Be quiet, old man. Jerusalem is ahead, and the Temple, and the Passover, and the Kingdom of God. Do not disturb the Master."

Who would have been surprised if someone among the disciples had said to Judas, "Reach into the bag and throw him a few coins, perhaps that will shut him up before the Master hears him."

But his cry will not be silenced. It slices through the hubbub of the crowd and irritates those who urge the procession along. Like a traffic light stuck on red the ridiculous beggar continues to cry, "Jesus, Son of David, have mercy on me."

It is written: "And Jesus stopped."

The timetable of eternity is involved. The day of final Passover approaches when the Lamb of God who takes away the sin of the world will be sacrificed.

But it is written: "And Jesus stopped."

But no matter. Jesus stops and the whole crowd stops with him, bumping into each other at the sudden, unexpected halt.

On his way to fulfill God's holy purpose long since foretold; on his way to accomplish the salvation of the world; on his way to be crowned on a cross Lord of the universe — and he stops at the cry for mercy from one obscure blind beggar sitting in the dust by the side of the road.

Jesus seems to be in no particular hurry. He asks that the beggar be brought to him. The one whom others try to ignore, Jesus calls to him.

"What do you want me to do for you?" Jesus asks. The one whom others try to silence, Jesus gives a chance to speak and to make his need known.

"Lord, let me receive my sight."

Perhaps the blind man sees more clearly than those around him who have eyes. For he believes that when Jesus of Nazareth is passing by the blind man himself can become a celestial stop sign on the road to salvation. He believes that although the journey has cosmic dimensions Jesus will not ignore the cry of the lowliest person on the edge of the crowd.

"Receive your sight. Your faith has made you well."

And immediately he received his sight. And followed him in the way, glorifying God.

The blind man, now restored, follows Jesus on the road, glorifying God. Time and again Jesus has issued the invitation, "Follow me." This journey from Galilee to Jerusalem has been a road of discipleship. Many have followed along the way, and now another joins the movement.

What has Jesus accomplished by halting at the celestial stop sign? He has brought an outsider, a blind beggar, out of obscurity and hopelessness into a new life and a new relationship. He has demonstrated that he cares for the least and the most helpless. He has heeded a cry for mercy and given a poor suppliant sight and wholeness. He has added another person to the company of his disciples, one who follows with gratitude and joy on the road to the Cross, giving glory to God.

It is good news to know that the one who leads the procession to Jerusalem to accomplish the salvation of the world will stop — even if the Cross must wait a while. He will stop at a cry for mercy; he will stop for a prayer for sight.

And since I am in dire need of both mercy and of sight, that makes me glad.

But there is one thing that bothers me a little.

I vaguely remember seeing a huddled figure sitting beside the road covered with a dusty mantle. But I was in a hurry. I had great things to do. So I moved on. I did not stop.

I wonder if I have run far too many celestial stop signs lately. What about you?

A Gift For One Who Has Everything

This sermon was prepared for a seminary congregation at a regular chapel service at Columbia Seminary.

It can be characterized as a public wrestling with the text as the preacher expresses his own sense of discomfort with the story. He resists identification with the man "who has everything" until he finally recognizes that he and the rich young ruler have more in common than he first thought.

By applying the passage most directly to his own experience, he hopes that the hearers will see themselves in the narrative.

A scholarly commentary says that the man who comes to Jesus in this story is not named so that every reader can identify with him.

Well, I find that rather difficult to do in my case. For traditionally, by harmonizing the synoptic account of this narrative, the man is known as the rich young ruler.

I find it somewhat incongruous to lay claim to any of these titles. And as for keeping all the commandments "from my youth," well, that takes in far too long a span of time for me. Since last Wednesday, perhaps, but hardly "from my youth."

So if I must identify with someone in this story, maybe I can try identifying with Jesus. But I quickly find that doesn't work either. For one thing, as soon as the man says to Jesus, "Teacher, all these I have observed from my youth," Mark, and only Mark, writes, "And Jesus, looking at him, loved him."

And I ask, "Why?"

I must admit that I am somewhat uneasy around people who never make a mistake, who seem always to have it all together, who always say exactly the right thing at the right time all the time, and who tell only of their successes because they are not aware of any failures.

Then, too, it seems to me that Jesus could have relaxed the conditions a little in the case of this young man.

I think if I had been screening recruits I would have said to this one (even if I didn't like him very much), "Come, follow me. Join us and bring your possessions with you, especially your checkbook and your billfold full of credit cards."

For a group led by someone who has no place to lay his head, for a bunch who is sent out taking "no bread, no bag, no money for your purses," it would be nice to have some reserves they can fall back on when they are in a tight spot.

So if I don't identify with the rich young ruler very well nor with Jesus, then that leaves me with the disciples "amazed at his word" and "exceedingly astonished." For if someone who has everything misses out on the Kingdom of God, where does that leave the likes of you and me?

At first glance this young man does seem to have everything. He is eager. He is courteous. He is reverent toward Jesus. He is concerned for his own spiritual welfare. He is morally good, upright, respectable. And he has great possessions. Most of us would be hard put to say to him, "You lack one thing."

But he himself senses that something is missing. He may not be as arrogant, cocky, and self-assured as he appears at first glance. As I look at him more closely I can come a little nearer understanding why; as "Jesus looked straight at him, his heart warmed to him," as the *New English Bible* translates it.

For there is a chink or two in that perfectly polished armor. There is a fermenting discontent, a reaching out, a thinly disguised cry for help in his question, "What must I do to inherit eternal life?"

It is as if he is saying in puzzled bewilderment, "Here I am, Lord, with all these abilities, talents, morality, security, and power. Surely there is something I can do to focus it all together so that life becomes complete and whole. What is it, Lord?"

There is a wistful vulnerability, a subtle sense of incompleteness in his "All these I have observed from my youth." This he has done, and still it is not enough to satisfy him.

Perhaps one reason Jesus' heart warms toward him is because this young man is so near to becoming a disciple. He is on the right road. He is concerned about the right thing — eternal life. He is living up to the light that he has. But he wants to take another step, to break out of the sameness and predictability of his strictly legal morality.

So he leaves himself open to Jesus' penetrating gaze and insightful probing.

Instead of saying to him, "You have everything," Jesus says, "You lack one thing."

In response to Jesus' word, the young man's heart must leap with hope. "Only one thing! Surely I can do that, or buy that, or earn that, so that I can slip it like a keystone into the arch of my life and all will be well."

But then ominous words come from Jesus: "Go — sell all — give."

Like hammer blows on a great gong the words reverberate through the labyrinths of his soul. "Go — sell — give!"

They so overwhelm him — as they do us — that he scarcely hears the last part of Jesus' words. He is too shaken to realize that Jesus is offering a gift to one who has everything.

He misses the promise, "You will have treasure in heaven."

He misses the gracious invitation, "Come; come share companionship and life with Jesus Christ."

He passes by the open challenge to a great adventure, "Follow me."

He misses the opportunity to be one of those who discovers that the road which leads to a cross ultimately leads to resurrection and new life.

He is too shaken to grasp that even the words "sell all" are a gift. The gift of letting go, of not having to parade credentials, without carrying anymore the burden of one who has everything.

But the gift of complete trust — not in self-achievement, self-possession, or self-fulfillment, but the gift of complete trust in God.

Jesus offers this man who has everything the gift of discipleship, and discipleship means letting go of one's predictable security and following Jesus Christ on whatever road he beckons.

The rich young ruler is too proud to accept a gift, for sometimes it takes more grace to accept a gift than to give one. Because he cannot let go, he has no hands free to grasp the gift Jesus offers him.

Now at last I am beginning to see that I am nearer to the rich young ruler than I thought, and so, most likely, are you.

For I find it difficult indeed to let go all the credentials for discipleship which I have built up all these years.

I cannot do it, Lord, unless you give me the gift of letting go so that my hands are free to receive the gift of yourself.

Luke 24:13-35

The Emmaus Road Revisited

The original date of the composition of this sermon is lost in the shadowy past. It was one of the first, if not the first I ever preached using the first person singular pronoun and speaking for one of the characters in the narrative. It was first preached at Covenant Presbyterian Church, Tuscaloosa, Alabama, probably in the early 1950s. It has been preached in a great variety of settings and churches since then.

I speak for the unnamed companion of Cleopas on the road to Emmaus. The sermon seeks to draw the hearers into the emotions of these two disciples as they walk with the Stranger who later reveals himself as the Risen Christ. One purpose of the sermon is to suggest to the congregation that Jesus can surprise us with his presence at unexpected times and places, but that he is especially near at the "breaking of bread."

Cleopas and I had walked the road from Emmaus to Jerusalem and back again many times, and the way had never seemed uncommonly long. But this time the road stretched out endlessly before us. The long day after the sabbath had finally dragged to a close. The shadows were creeping forward in languid lengths. We should have quickened our pace and hurried along our way in order to reach home before the sun had set. But what did it matter if darkness caught us on the way? What did anything matter anymore? For us and for a handful like us the sun had set long since. An eerie, crushing darkness had enveloped us three days before. And now, although the light of the sun was still bright upon the road, we were like men groping, stumbling in the dark, feeling our way along a much traveled path, but now strange, unmarked, and

91

unfamiliar. But why hurry home? What would be there? A dark house, a dead candle on the table, and tasteless bread.

But we could not walk in silence. We talked. We talked about the past, about yesterday, and the day before, and the day before that. I say we talked, but mostly we asked each other questions. Not that I expected Cleopas to have the answers, nor did he expect the same of me. It was simply a way of expressing the hurt, despair, and frustration each of us felt.

Most of our questions could be summed up in the one word, "Why?" Why had this Man whom we had come to call Master and who had spoken so confidently of God, and love, and overcoming the world let himself be overcome by the hate of the high priests and the stupidity of the Romans and the rabble? Peter told us that on the night he was arrested the Master had spent hours in prayer as if pleading for his Father's help, but when the temple guards came to take him he offered no resistance. When Peter struck out with his sword, Jesus seemed more annoyed with Peter than with Judas, who had led the police to his place of prayer.

And at the trial, he who had argued in the temple, confounded the scribes with his simple eloquence, and fearlessly driven the money changers from the Court of the Gentiles stood meek and almost speechless, making no defense. What few words he did say did not help his cause, nor ours. He practically admitted to the charge of blasphemy and sedition, but did not really explain what he meant by "Son of God" or "Son of Man" or his "kingdom."

Why had he who had performed such mighty works as making the blind to see, the lame to walk, and the dead to rise let himself be nailed to a cross and crucified as a common criminal? Why had he not met the challenge of the high priest and come down from the cross? Then they as well as we would have known that he was who we wanted him to be.

So we plodded along, asking each other our unanswerable questions, trying to put as much distance as possible between ourselves and Jerusalem and thus perhaps to begin to forget what had happened there. Jerusalem, the Holy City — I did not care if I ever saw the place again, Temple or no Temple.

But as we walked I began to feel that we were not alone. There was the sense of Another's presence. I felt that it was not Cleopas only who was hearing my questions, but that Another was listening.

I had heard no distant footsteps, but there was still the awareness of being followed. Once I looked back over my shoulder, but the road to Jerusalem was empty. Then the feeling grew into a reality. There was Someone else traveling with us on the road. At first he said not a word. He simply suited his pace to ours, and we walked together. But for all the strangeness of his being there I felt no fear. I did not stop to ask where he came from nor how he came to overtake us when neither of us had seen him coming. It seemed right that he should walk beside us.

He listened for a while, and then he spoke, "What is this about which you are talking?"

We stood still and looked at him in amazement. Surely anyone who had been in Jerusalem for Passover would know from words like Sanhedrin, Pilate, Jesus, and crucifixion what we were talking about. What else was there to talk about?

So Cleopas, almost impatiently, said to him, "You must be the only visitor to Jerusalem who does not know what has been going on there."

Then the stranger said, "What things?"

For a fleeting moment I caught a flash in his eye which said to me, "This man is asking not so much for information but to see what things we think are important."

Well, we began to tell him. We were so intent to tell him that our words tumbled over each other and our sentences clashed against each other like crossed swords.

It never occurred to us that the man might be a temple spy sent to hunt out the friends of the Crucified. It never crossed our minds that what we were saying identified us to a perfect stranger as followers of one condemned. It seemed right and natural that we should tell him our deepest thoughts and reveal our shattered, broken hopes. For he listened with an intensity which made us know that he had ears which really hear.

We told him of Jesus of Nazareth and how we had been convinced by his words, his deeds, the mysterious majesty of his very person that he was the promised Messiah and that in him all the hopes of God's visiting and redeeming his people had been centered. We told him with both grief and anger how he had been betrayed, tried, condemned, and crucified. We told him how he had died on a cross between two thieves, an agonizing, horrible, lonely death, exposed and naked to the taunts and jeers of his enemies, and helpless to ease the anguish or dry the tears of his friends.

We told him of the ridiculous rumors some excitable women of our company had spread — that his tomb this very morning was empty and that angels — angels, mind you — had appeared to them saying that he is alive.

The part about the empty tomb we believed, for this was confirmed by some of the men. But there are many ways to empty a grave. We took it as the last indignity heaped upon him. His enemies were not content to let him rest even in his grave.

But alive? If this were true — and how could it be? — then where is he? If he had been raised then surely he would have strode into the very Court of the Temple and startled the High Priest and the Sanhedrin out of their wits and proved them wrong. He would have gone to Pilate's palace, stood face to face with the trembling governor, and said, "You asked me, 'What is truth?' Then look at me. The truth is that the might of Rome cannot defeat the Messiah of the God of Israel."

But none of these things had happened. The tomb was empty, true enough, but what matter? It was no more empty than our hearts; no more empty than all the dreary days ahead of us.

For a moment the Stranger was silent as if to see if indeed we had any more to say. Then he began to speak. Of course, I expected him to speak smooth words of comfort, to share our sorrow, to seek to ease our pain. But instead his words were strong, his voice vibrant with an underlying tone of impatience.

"Oh foolish people, and slow of heart to believe all that the prophets have spoken."

Then without a scroll in his hand he began to show us from our own scriptures, beginning with Genesis and going through the prophets, how all through our history God had never let his people go; how time and again God had overruled the cruel purposes of tyrants to redeem his people. In the time of Moses, the Lord, by a mighty hand, mocked the might of Pharaoh of Egypt to bring about a new beginning for the people of Israel. From the prophets he showed us how God's Chosen One was meant to be the Suffering Servant, giving himself fully for his people, but never finally forsaken by God who as sovereign Creator can bring life out of the darkness of death.

I considered myself something of a student of the Writings, but never had I seen them in such a light before; never had they made so much sense; never had I grasped in both hands at once the mysterious holiness and the yearning, suffering love of God. Even the tragedy of the bloody cross began to take its place in the perspective of God's purpose. I could even hope that the rumors of a Risen Christ might indeed be true.

As he talked we were not aware of how quickly we had covered the last few miles to home. Suddenly we stood before our door in Emmaus, and the sun was almost set. The Stranger made no move to tarry with us. But we could not let him go alone into the night, so we urged him to stay.

"Abide with us," we said, "for it is toward evening, and the day is far spent."

Without hesitation he came in with us. We felt no need to make excuses for our humble home nor to explain that we had been away for days and therefore everything was not in perfect order. We knew he understood and would accept things as they were. Quickly we prepared a simple meal and the three of us sat down at table together.

For some reason neither Cleopas nor I felt that we should act as host. Quite naturally, without ostentation, the Stranger was the host. He took the bread and said the prayer of blessing. He broke the bread; broke it with strong authority and gave it to us.

And then it happened!

In that moment we knew him! Do not ask me how we knew; we simply knew. Something about his voice, perhaps; the way he prayed; the mystery he made of a simple act like breaking bread. It could be no one else but he; no one but our Master with whom we had shared bread before.

Indeed he was alive and so were we.

But as suddenly as we knew that he was with us, he was gone; that is, we could not see him. But there was no sense of loss, no crushing loneliness. There was an exhilarating joy, a sense of new life, an overwhelming urgency to share, to tell someone that it is true. He is the Christ, and he is alive!

Without finishing our meal we were out the door and on the road again, on the road to Jerusalem, the Holy City, from which only a few hours before we had tried to escape. The long and weary road, but a road soon covered by running, leaping steps.

We found the others in the upper room. They sat in wonder, for they, too, had heard the news, and that from Peter. We felt no disappointment that we were not the first bearers of good tidings. We were too intent to tell them of how he had come to us, had followed us when we were trying to escape, had listened, and spoken, and then made himself known in the breaking of bread. The dead-end road to Emmaus had become for us the way to resurrection life.

Never again will we walk that road, nor any other, but in the assurance that he walks with us. Never again will we read the sacred Writings but that his voice will speak to us through them. Never again will we come home at the end of the weary day to an empty house, a dead candle on the table, and tasteless bread. But also he will be there to bless and break the bread and make himself known.

Well, my friends of nineteen centuries after me, that is my story. I know you have your Emmaus Roads, too, which seem beset with doubts and fears and broken hopes. But let me tell you this good news: Jesus Christ is as alive today as when he walked the road with us. And he wants to walk your road, too. With him beside you, your Emmaus Road can become the way of resurrection.

Deductive And Inductive Sermons

The processes of deduction and induction are mirror opposites. In deduction a principle, theme, or general conclusion is stated at the outset, followed by supporting data such as examples, illustrations, or statistics. In induction the data comes first and leads to or points toward a general conclusion or conclusions. One form of the inductive method aims progressively toward a single, increasingly self-evident conclusion. A different form places more value on the process of exploration and invites a variety of conclusions along the way and at the journey's end. In either case, however, the data and the process invite parallel thinking, pointing not backward to a previously stated premise but forward to one or more emerging implications.

In preaching, the deductive method shapes a sermon in several particular ways. A theme or central idea is established as predominant early in the sermon. The sermon then develops this theme or idea through sub-themes or clearly differentiated points. When stories are used, they serve as illustrations that prove the validity of the themes or points. The three sermons that I have designated as deductive are "This Above All," "Thank God And Take Courage," and "Foundations."

"This Above All" is a first-rate example of classic deductive construction. It begins with a description of the contemporary context, the situation in which the members of the congregation find themselves. The sermon then focuses its theme in a relevant question "which has erupted suddenly in our midst and turned the eyes of the whole world upon us." Here the relevant question is "Where is the final authority?" In this particular sermon this question immediately spins itself into a series of restatements and related questions. Yet the single question, as the sermon's guiding theme, remains central, "Where is the final authority?"

In contrast to some stereotypes of the deductive sermon, this sermon does not leave the members of the congregation detached by appealing only to their minds. Rather it draws them into its sphere of influence as they recognize their involvement in the "present crisis" and claim the question as their own. The sermon makes explicit the relevancy of the theme of authority to the lives of those who make up the congregation.

In classic deductive preaching a sermon's beginning or introduction gives three pieces of information: the sermon's theme or central idea, the relevance of this theme or idea to the congregation's contemporary situation, and the scripture on which the sermon will build. Any one, and on rare occasions two, of these pieces of information can be delayed to the middle or the end of the sermon. But normally these three — theme, relevance, and scripture — form the triumvirate that governs the classic deductive sermon from the sermon's beginning.

In "This Above All" once the relevance is clear, even before the sermon's theme is stated and restated in question form, Ormond claims that Romans 13 "has some clear and definite things to say to us." Thus, as the sermon's and the congregation's questions clamor for response, Romans 13 holds out the promise of answers. Ormond's commitment to the norm of stating the scripture passage early in the sermon can be inferred from a comment in his introduction to "When Remembering Is More Than Reminiscence," a comment that seems to highlight an aberration or a variation on an expected pattern: "The scripture text itself is not dealt with directly until at the conclusion of the sermon."

At this point in the sermon — with the theme, relevance, and scriptural base clear — the sermon could still take an inductive turn were it to engage in a search for the anticipated answer and delay a statement of that answer until near the end of the sermon. Instead, in good deductive fashion, this sermon immediately turns to scripture for "the Christian's position" which is "abundantly clear." And continuing in good deductive fashion, the body of the sermon elaborates this Christian position with reference both to Romans 13 and the contemporary situation. The sermon's three points can be summarized in three imperatives: obey the laws of the land, love your neighbor as yourself, and "this above all — put on the Lord Jesus Christ." Here in the sermon's body Ormond shows himself to be a master craftsman. The three points are not interchangeable. Rather they build, each being a higher calling than the one previous. The third section then is the apex of the sermon. Explicit in this third section is the claim that in Jesus Christ are found answers "to the complexities of our problems of race," the context of the sermon's relevance to the congregation's lives as stated in the sermon's beginning. Implicit in this third section is the claim that Jesus Christ is the final authority, the sermon's theme. The sermon's conclusion consists of two appeals to the congregation that grow out of this third section's focus on the preeminence of Jesus Christ. The final three sentences of the sermon return to the difficulty of the contemporary situation, recalling the sermon's beginning. The sermon ends with good news, the promise of Christ's presence in the worshipers' daily lives.

Ormond is no slave to form. He shapes the form to his own ends. As this sermon draws to a close, Ormond introduces a significant variation on the standard pattern. The standard pattern that underlies this sermon's shape is as follows: the beginning that introduces the triumvirate of relevance, scripture, and theme, and that crystallizes both relevance and theme in a relevant question which scripture promises to answer; the body of the sermon that consists of three points, each drawn from the scripture passage and each clarifying and applying to life an answer to the initial relevant question; and the conclusion that makes a specific appeal or appeals based on the body of the sermon and relevant to the congregation's lives.

Ormond varies this pattern as he nears the end of his sermon. The claim that in Jesus Christ are the answers to the current perplexing questions raises the ineluctable question, "Why have the answers not been found before now?" In four brief sentences Ormond repeats his entire sermon structure. That is, he follows his second relevant question with its answer, a brief description of "two reasons." Answer immediately follows question. The two reasons then issue directly in the sermon's final appeals to the congregation — "seek to know Christ more intimately" and pray for forgiveness.

Ormond's form here with its variation serves his content. The sermon begins by bringing to the forefront disturbing tensions; the sermon exposes "the complex web of conflicting forces in which we are caught." Using a deductive approach, Ormond answers the tension and complexity with scriptural truth claims, which he develops through definition, application, and exhortation. By words and structure he seeks to establish certainty in the midst of complexity. But the tension he describes is deep; it cannot be explained away; it is felt tension; it is real and disturbing. Perhaps Ormond intuits that one round of question and answer is insufficient. So he goes round again with a new question and an old answer, Jesus Christ. The sermon by its content and its deductive form seeks to establish Jesus as a rock in a time of troublin'.

"Thank God And Take Courage" also evidences a deductive approach, particularly in its use of narrative material. The sermon's beginning, similar in its broad strokes to "This Above All," sets the sermon within a specific contemporary context and focuses the sermon's theme, thanksgiving as "genuine gratitude." Missing here, however, is an introduction of the scripture passage, which is delayed until the middle of the sermon.

The body of the sermon follows a deductive pattern in two ways. First it begins with an extended definition of "genuine thanksgiving." The general precedes the particular; the statement of a principle or truth claim precedes its supporting evidence. After defining his understanding of true thanksgiving, Ormond then turns to scripture for examples that illustrate and confirm this understanding. Here is a second characteristic of the deductive approach: stories serve to support a previously stated truth claim.

It is possible to divide the body of this sermon into three principal parts: one, the definition of genuine thanksgiving; two, an example of such thanksgiving from Paul's life that demonstrates his giving thanks in the face of "the reality of life in this world"; and, three, an example from the life of Paul that both demonstrates his ability to give thanks in the face of adversity and presents others as the unwitting occasion for his thankfulness. Notice that here the "points" are not equals like I, II, III on an outline; nor are they interchangeable. They function less like points and more like "moves," to use David Buttrick's language.[5] They are broad sections of the sermon's body that move the sermon from its beginning to its end. Ormond turns section one, the definition, into a premise with two halves which, he says, he will validate with biblical evidence; section two, the portrait of Paul drawn from his letters, functions as supporting evidence for one-half of the premise; section three, the extended story of Paul's journey to Rome, is a more complete example, constituting supporting evidence for both halves of the premise.

The sermon's conclusion returns to the context described in its beginning, "Thanksgiving week, 1983." Based on the insights of the sermon's body, the sermon challenges the congregation to give particular thanks for the Church and for Jesus Christ. The sermon then concludes with good news, Jesus Christ who "comes out to meet us" and makes thanksgiving possible.

"Foundations" is noteworthy because of its clear outline-type structure, like a cumulative argument of a well-written essay. There are three major sections — each a foundational doctrine for the Presbyterian church. Each section builds upon what has gone before: the first foundation "leads us to the second foundation"; the first and second "lead us to the third foundation." The development of each section is also carefully arranged. The outline is fairly explicit:

I. Introduction — the context and the theme: three primary Presbyterian doctrines
II. Body
    A. Foundation #1 — Jesus is Lord
       1. What do we mean by these words? Answer
       2. Why is he Lord?
          a. answer #1, who he is in his person
          b. what this answer does not mean
          c. answer #4, what he has done
       3. What does this Lordship mean for the church?
          a. answer
          b. the difficulty of this Lordship
       4. How are we to know the will of the Lord?
          (This question leads to B.)

B. Foundation #2 — The Authority of Scripture
   1. What this means for officers in the church
   2. What this means about reading Scripture
      (Foundations #1 and #2 lead to C.)
C. Foundation #3 — The Unity of the Church
   1. How #1 leads to #3
   2. How #2 leads to #3
III. Conclusion — reminder of the context and the doctrines

In this sermon Ormond illustrates Long's advice to divide the "larger tasks into smaller components" (Long 1989, p. 107).

Although "This Above All," "Thank God And Take Courage," and "Foundations" are far richer and far more complex than these brief, limited descriptions indicate, the deductive tenor of each sermon is paramount. They, therefore, provide definite points of contrast with four other sermons which evidence an inductive approach, "The Celestial Stop Sign," "A Gift For One Who Has Everything," "The Emmaus Road Revisited," and "A Sermon In Clay" (found in the previous section with the story sermons).

A clear point of contrast is the use of story in "Thank God And Take Courage" and in "The Celestial Stop Sign." As I have already said, "Thank God And Take Courage" uses the story of Paul's journey to Rome deductively — the story's meaning is controlled by the truth claim that has already been stated and that the story aims to illustrate and confirm. "The Celestial Stop Sign" uses its two stories inductively — meanings emerge as the stories unfold and Ormond spells out his understandings of the stories after both have been told. These two sermons demonstrate how from one point of view induction and deduction are mirror opposites. It is interesting that in each of these sermons there are two truth claims that in one are supported by the use of story and in the other are drawn from the pair of stories.

From another point of view, however, induction and deduction are not mirror opposites in that their use of stories demands different responses from the members of the congregation.[6] The deductive approach sets their ears for discerning meaning. Meaning is explicitly prescribed and the congregation's proper response to a story as supporting evidence is a "Yes, that clarifies, or confirms, or deepens, or broadens my understanding and experience of the issue at hand." The inductive approach risks the congregation's drawing unexpected meanings from a story. Although the preacher exercises considerable control over a story's meaning through the use of narrative techniques such as point of view, character portrayal, and in delivery tone of voice, the congregation is plunged into the narrative with no explicit clues as to the meaning or meanings the preacher has discerned or imbedded in it. Therefore, the members of the congregation are free to "think [their] own thoughts and experience [their] own feelings" (Craddock 1979, p. 157) and potentially to arrive at conclusions that differ from the preacher's. Some tellers of tales welcome a variety of inter-pretations. One writer of children's stories considers the readers to be "coauthors" (Paterson 1989, p. 37). She writes:

> *It's a wonderful feeling when readers hear what I thought I was trying to say, but there is no law that they must. Frankly, it is even more thrilling for a reader to find something in my writing that I hadn't until that moment known was there.* (Paterson 1981, p. 24)

Whether a sermon aims for the members of the congregation to arrive at precisely its conclusion,[7] or whether it invites multiple responses, the inductive use of stories always gives them consider-able freedom in discerning meanings as they experience the story and sometimes run ahead of it in their efforts to understand it and apply it to their lives. In one reading of "The Celestial Stop Sign," I found myself praying, "Dear God, give me sight." My prayer came just before Ormond's sentence, "And since I am in dire need of both mercy and of sight, that makes me glad." An inductive use of stories invites such running ahead of the preacher as the mem-bers of the congregation lay their own lives beside the story and draw personal conclusions.

In "The Celestial Stop Sign" Ormond's use of stories makes the sermon's shape inductive. There is no formal introduction. The sermon begins with the opening story; its middle is a second, lengthier story, a retelling of the scripture passage that echoes motifs, events, and themes from the first story; it ends with two implications for life suggested by the stories. Unlike the two deductive sermons discussed above, here there is no early announcement of the sermon's theme; nor is there an explicit statement of the sermon's relevance to life until the end, although points of relevance are implied as the second story unfolds. Here also there is no declaration of the purpose for turning to scripture. Ormond does not alert the members of the congregation that he is turning to scripture for answers or examples. Instead the scripture passage is presented purely as a story that promises, as does any story, to offer up meaning in its telling. There is a slightly new triumvirate in inductive preaching — relevance to life, scripture, and meanings for the preacher that evoke meanings in the congregation. I believe it is essential to inductive preaching that all three be present by the end of the sermon. Sometimes meanings for the preacher and connections to life remain implicit as oblique hints that leave the sermon's conclusion to the congregation; sometimes they are explicitly stated and in such cases they are normally reserved until near the sermon's end.

The common shape that governs both "The Celestial Stop Sign" and "A Gift For One Who Has Everything" is, I believe, more helpfully identified as a plot than as a formal essay or argument. Thus, these particular sermons could also be identified as "narrative."[8] The plot of "The Celestial Stop Sign" is straightforward, consisting of a beginning, a middle, and an end[9] as three distinct sections. The plot of "A Gift For One Who Has Everything" is more intricate. There is a beginning, middle, and end, but the middle is complex with a twist, a turn, a doubling back.

In "A Gift For One Who Has Everything" Ormond is a fine storyteller as well as preacher. Like Craddock with his inductive approach to preaching, Ormond in this sermon charts his wrestling with the text and his arrival at its meaning for his life (Craddock 1979, pp. 123-26). Like Eugene Lowry with his narrative approach to preaching, Ormond in this sermon moves "from disequilibrium to resolution" (Lowry 1985, p. 52). My description here evidences my indebtedness to both Craddock and Lowry.

Within two sentences "A Gift For One Who Has Everything" has identified a problem, trouble, mind disequilibrium — all words Lowry uses to describe the narrative sermon's beginning. In this sermon the trouble is that the preacher is unable to identify with the appropriate character in the biblical story. An implied question arises: With whom in this story can the preacher, and by implication the congregation, identify?[10] The sermon begins with a "no" answer, a false resolution: the rich young ruler is not an option. In search of resolution, the sermon explores a second option, identification with Jesus. This option also proves to be a false resolution, leaving the implied question still hanging. Still searching for resolution, the sermon tries a third option, the disciples. Here Ormond finds a fit, a "Yes," true resolution.[11]

There immediately arises, however, a new problem. To identify with the disciples is to be "amazed" and "astonished" at Jesus' response to the rich young ruler. The problem is, what is wrong with this man that he "misses out on the Kingdom of God"? This is no academic question. If *he* doesn't make it, what about "the likes of you and me"? The resolution to the first problem creates new, felt disequilibrium. At this point in the sermon Ormond reveals his craftsmanship: the second problem does not send the sermon off in a new direction. Ormond does not introduce a second problem that needs a second resolution. Instead at this point the sermon begins to double back on itself. Resolving the second problem involves re-evaluating the character of the ruler. This re-evaluation results in a retelling of the biblical story. This retelling leads to a re-evaluation of the opening false resolution. The preacher, perhaps along with the congregation, discovers an affinity between himself and the ruler. The sermon has returned to its beginning with a twist; the initial "No" has become an uncomfortable "Yes." Reluctantly, repentantly, Ormond acknowledges his affinity with the ruler, an acknowledgment that forces from his lips the simple, heartfelt prayer of confession with which the sermon closes. In one short sentence prayer, the inductive triumvirate comes together — scripture, relevance to life, and meaning in the preacher's life. The prayer is an invitation to the congregation to whisper an echoing prayer. The prayer is also a reminder of the good news that the Lord who makes demands is also the gift-giver who makes obedience possible. The sermon's narrative movement has come to "a proper ending," gospel resolution.[12] The sermon's inductive movement, having recreated "the experience of arriving at a conclusion" (Craddock 1979, p. 125), now leaves the congregation "to their own decisions and conclusion" (*Ibid.*, p. 146).

Both "The Celestial Stop Sign" and "A Gift For One Who Has Everything" might be called directed inductive preaching. Both direct the members of the congregation toward a specific response — in the former, remembering and looking for the celestial stop signs in their lives; in the latter, claiming the closing prayer for themselves.

"The Emmaus Road Revisited" is also directed inductive preaching. Although it is pure story, as a first-person narrative, the sermon's express aim is given in the last three sentences where the story-sermon is directly applied to the worshiping community's life. As I reread this sermon, however, evocative language and implicit connections between the story and life elicited meanings in my heart and mind long before the sermon's ending. Jesus "listened with an intensity which made us know that he had ears which really hear." Thoughts and memories and emotions spin around my heart and mind: How often have my ears been deaf? How often have I listened but not with such intensity? Can I remember the last time when I did listen with intensity, with ears which really hear? "In that moment we knew him! ... Something about ... the mystery he made of a simple act like breaking bread." Those words drew from me an uncomfortable memory of my own uninspired attempts to be celebrant. How might I capture something of that mystery when I break the bread at my next communion? Inductive preaching deliberately invites the congregation to make their own connections with the sermon. The directed inductive approach seeks to lead the worshipers to the particular conclusion with which the sermon closes.

"A Sermon In Clay," also discussed previously with the story-sermons, adopts a more open-ended inductive approach. The narrative that constitutes the sermon, coupled with the two passages of scripture, merely hints at meanings. Connections, relevance, meanings remain oblique and, therefore, become the responsibility of the congregation. Along a spectrum of inductive preaching, "The Celestial Stop Sign" and "A Gift For One Who Has Everything" belong near one end where a sermon intentionally seeks to evoke a limited range of meanings. "A Sermon In Clay" belongs near the opposite end of the spectrum where "it is the privilege of the reader [or worshiper] to discover what a book [or sermon] means for his or her particular life" (Paterson 1989, p. 15). On this end of the spectrum the reader/worshiper is plunged "to his or her own emotional and imaginative roots and makes connections the author herself [or the preacher] wouldn't have dreamed of" (*Ibid.*, p. 69).

The sermons discussed in this section are both inspirational and instructive. I hope I have not simply described and dissected, but more importantly elucidated and issued an invitation. My hope in analyzing these sermons has been to pave the way for students and preachers to try their hand at designing similar types of sermons. A deductive sermon has, in general, a certain set of characteristics and a certain feel. An inductive sermon has, in general, a different set of characteristics and a different feel. There is no surefire method of learning to preach or expanding one's homiletical repertoire. I invite us all, myself included, to the slow, sometimes painful, method of experimentation and apprenticeship to a master preacher.

Sermons By
Other Templates

Remember The Loaves

It is obvious that this sermon was prepared for a seminary congregation. It was part of a communion service in the Columbia Seminary chapel a few days before the end of the academic year. I was struck by the irony in Mark's narrative. Mark recounts "on the same page" the feeding by Jesus of 4,000 people with a meager supply of bread. The disciples experienced this abundant feeding, but still they are concerned because they forget to bring bread for their journey. The one loaf they do bring seems woefully inadequate.

Jesus reminds them of two occasions when he fed a multitude with very few loaves. Have they forgotten how much food was left over after these feedings?

The sermon is designed to remind us of how often we, too, forget the abundant supply of grace which Christ gives us. The Lord's Supper is a symbol of meeting great hunger with a small amount of literal food. It is an invitation to remember the loaves of God's grace.

It is your first Sunday at the church where you are to spend your summer of supervised ministry. The service is going pretty well, you think, although you were a little nervous when you read the Old Testament lesson and stumbled a little over the name, Melchizedek. You did knock the hymnbook off the chair when you went back to sit down, but the carpet on the chancel floor muffled the sound. You were careful to wait until everybody's eyes were closed for a prayer before you picked it up.

Right now you are trying to listen to the minister preach. He really speaks well and sounds confident and sincere. You are sure that you will learn a lot from him about preaching. But it is a little hard to listen because you keep having this feeling that everybody is looking at you as you sit in the big chair to the left of the pulpit. You see two teenagers whispering to each other, and although you know from not so distant experience what teenagers whisper about, you are certain that they are whispering about you as if you could hear their very words.

Finally the service is over, and you are standing at the door with the pastor. Some people hurry by without a glance in your direction. But several stop, shake your hand, smile, and tell you they are glad you are here. Some express specific offers of help and encouragement.

After all have passed by and the minister has said a kind word to you, you make your way down the hall to the unused Sunday school room you have claimed for a study. But on the way you pass the room where the deacons are counting the offering. Through a half-opened door you overhear a conversation.

"Well, what do you think of this one?"

"Let's hope she is better than the one we had last summer. At least I could understand what she said when she read the scripture. That fellow last summer sounded as if he had a mouth full of grits when he preached."

"But you have to admit that he got better before the summer was over. But I'm not so sure about this one. She seems mighty young, and a woman at that. I don't know quite yet how I feel about a woman in the pulpit. I may just go fishing on the days she is scheduled to preach."

You go on down to your unused classroom, close the door, and sink into the secondhand office chair.

"Why am I here? What have I gotten myself into? Did I forget to bring bread?"

You search through the thoughts and dreams and hopes and expectations of the process which brought you here. And you ask, "Where is the bread?"

Or you are the supervising pastor at this church. You have been here about five years. You have no pressing urge to move on to another place. Things are moving along well with the church. You and your family are happy here.

You feel unusually good about this morning's service, especially the sermon. You wish all of them went as well. You could sense the communication between yourself and the congregation.

After the service many made comments which went beyond the usual, "I enjoyed it." Some said, "You really spoke to me this morning." Some were silent, but pressed your hand a little harder than usual. You do wonder why the new summer intern did not comment on the sermon. You thought she would be impressed. Oh well, she was a little uptight today. Perhaps she will say something later in the week.

Sunday lunch is over, and you take a quick look at the paper. You are about to fall asleep in the chair when the phone rings with a shrill urgency. There is a voice cracking with emotion.

"Charlie, you've got to get over to Jim and Nancy's house right away. There has been a terrible accident on the highway. Their son, Michael, was killed. A drunk driver crossed the median and hit him head-on."

Your stomach contracts into a churning knot. Your throat feels as if someone is choking you. You search frantically for the car keys, and at last you are on your way.

"Michael, why Michael?" you keep muttering. "That fine, brilliant, promising boy. Why Michael? What will I say? What can I do?"

Then a slight shiver of consolation runs down your spine.

"Well, if anyone can handle this it is Jim and Nancy. I've never known anyone with a stronger faith than they have, especially Jim. They will probably handle this better than I will."

You roll to a jerking stop in front of the house and practically run up the walk. You do not wait to ring the bell. You go right in the front door, and there they are — Jim and Nancy and a few neighbors.

Jim's face is drawn and drained and he suddenly looks old. His dark eyes look up at you with cold hardness. He almost snarls through clinched teeth. "Tell me, Charlie, where was that shepherd God you talked about this morning? Where was he at 3:00 this afternoon out on that highway?"

The knot in your stomach comes back, and the invisible hand on your throat tightens. You wonder, "Have I forgotten to bring bread? Oh, God, we are starving here. Where is the bread?"

Or you are simply an ordinary Christian, if there is such a thing as an ordinary Christian. There is no spectacular crisis in your life, but neither is there any overwhelming joy. Day follows day as if each were cut from the same celestial cookie cutter, except that some have more ragged edges than others. Lately your faith has seemed more routine than real, more by rote than by conviction. The zest has gone out of it. It is not that you have any shattering doubts; it is simply that you seem to be groping for new questions and you are not sure what they are.

So another morning comes and you eat the ubiquitous bowl of soggy corn flakes with a little oat bran added for fiber. You drink your usual cup of black coffee. You pick up your briefcase which you brought home last night but never opened. You go out into the young day.

"Hello, world. Here I am again, but I wonder if I have forgotten to bring bread. Do I have enough bread to get me through this day?"

The Lord must be a God of infinite patience, for he has been listening to questions such as these from his people for eons.

How long has the ship of the church been rocking on the sea of the world with disciples in it who have forgotten to bring bread, and who say to one another plaintively, "We have no bread"?

His answer comes, "Why do you discuss the fact that you have no bread? Do you not yet perceive or understand? Having eyes do you not see, and having ears do you not hear? And do you not remember?"

Student intern: Do you not remember other times when you were afraid, and unsure, and overwhelmed, but you got through it? You knew you made it, not because of anything you consciously did, but because there was a presence.

Seasoned pastor, facing a devastated friend's searching question: Do you not remember that Another cried out at 3:00 in the afternoon, "My God, my God, why have you forsaken me?" Do you not remember that you have shared grief with God's people

114

many times before, and later they told you that they did not know how they would have made it without you? But you know it was not you who got them through, but the risen Christ who stood with you and with them.

Routine, everyday Christian, my brother or sister under the skin: Do you not remember? Why do you keep thinking about your own weariness and inadequacies and the regularity of the daily round, instead of remembering the loaves, the abundance of the loaves which the Lord has provided for you through all these years?

What better time and place to remember the loaves than at the Table of the Lord. One reason we return to this Table again and again is that we so easily forget. It is not that we forget the proper words or that Christ's body was broken for us. Rather it is that we need repeatedly to remember the loaves in such a way that our remembering helps us grasp in the present the reality of our Lord's giving himself on our behalf.

At this table it can always be said, "And they ate and were satisfied, and there were baskets full of grace left over."

Is Confession Too Easy?

This sermon was preached in the Columbia Seminary Chapel only a few weeks before my retirement from the faculty. It is addressed specifically to the issue of worship at the seminary. It deals with a concern of my own; I am not sure it was a concern of many others in the congregation.

I had come to sense that, at least for me, the repetition of formal printed prayers of confession was beginning to become routine and somewhat meaningless. This sermon may be an example of the preacher preaching more to himself than to the congregation.

It begins with a personal experience from my childhood, and relates that to a passage from 1 John.

When I was four years old — and I know some of you think that must have been around the turn of the century — I had the potential of becoming a first-class kleptomaniac.

My parents and I lived in a big house out in the country about three miles from a very small town in Sumter County, Alabama. Although the town was little it had what I thought was a great big store. In fact, we called it a department store, for unlike the general stores of the time and territory it had things arranged in departments. There was a clothing department, a dry goods department, a hardware department, a grocery department, and a toy department.

One day I was in the store with my parents. While we were doing some shopping I wandered off by myself and found the toy department. And there a particular article caught my eye. Just why I was attracted to this item I do not know, but I have been told that kleptomaniacs take things not because they need them, but for the sheer exhilaration of stealing and getting away with it.

The thing was a small, straight chair about eighteen inches high, made of wood, and painted white. I think it had a price tag of 25¢. It was too small and not strong enough for me to sit in, but I liked it anyway. So while no one was looking, I picked it up and walked off with it. Why my parents did not notice it when I returned to them, I do not know, unless it was that I was careful to walk behind them and hold the chair behind my back. Soon it was time to go home, so we left the store and climbed into the Model-T Ford with my father behind the wheel, my mother on the seat beside him, and me in the back with the "hot" chair on the floor under my feet.

My parents did not notice the chair until we were in the house.

"Where did you get that chair?" my father asked, suspiciously.

"At the store," I replied, innocently.

Then my mother asked a question to which I knew she knew the answer, for she knew I had no money.

"Did you pay for it?"

"No," I said, cockily. "I just took it."

Stunned silence filled the room. I could tell by the expression on my parents' faces that I had done something terribly wrong.

The next thing I expected to happen was that my mother would go out into the yard, break a long and supple limb from the peach tree, strip it of its leaves, bring it back into the house and burn up my bare legs with that switch. She had done so for far smaller offenses. But she did not do that. In fact, neither of my parents raised their voices to me. I suppose they were so shocked after all their good efforts, their only son was growing up to be a thief that they were speechless.

Several alternatives for action lay before us, and I shall mention them in the descending order of their appeal to me. The one which made most sense to me was for my father to drive back into town, take the chair to the salesperson in the toy department, and say nonchalantly, "My little boy bought one of those 25¢ chairs here this afternoon, but he forgot to pay for it. Here's your quarter."

This would have shifted the burden of my sin onto my father and relieved me of all responsibility and consequences.

But we didn't do that.

The next best thing from my point of view was for my mother to take the chair back into town, find the salesperson, and say with a nervous laugh, "My little boy bought this chair here this afternoon, but he has decided he does not want it, so I have brought it back."

This would have put my mother between me and the offended party and I would not have to admit to my sin. It never occurred to me what my mother would have done if the salesperson offered her a refund.

But we did not do that either.

The third alternative would involve all three of us. All of us would go back to the store. But before we got there my father would give me a quarter. I would go to the salesperson and say confidently, "I bought this chair here this afternoon, but I could not find anybody to give the money to, so here is your quarter."

Thus I would have covered one sin with another — a lie.

But we did not do that either.

What we did was, we all got into the car, my father behind the wheel, my mother on the seat beside him, and I in the back with the chair held firmly across my knees. When we got to the store all three of us went in, but my parents put me several paces in front of them. They followed as I made my way to the toy department with that chair held in full view for everybody to see.

I found the salesperson, held out the chair and said, "I took this chair this afternoon, but I did not pay for it. So I have brought it back. I am sorry that I took it."

The salesperson looked at me quizzically, took the chair and said simply, "Well, thank you for bringing it back."

We left the store and got into the car for the long ride home with my father behind the wheel, my mother beside him on the front seat, and me in the back seat crumpled in a corner like a discarded ball of tissue paper and feeling like Public Enemy Number One.

My parents never mentioned the incident again, and you can be sure that I never brought it up. Can you imagine in later years the three of us sitting around the fire reminiscing about my childhood and my saying, "Ha, ha! Do you remember the time I stole the chair?"

I don't think confession has ever come harder to me than it did that day. But I can tell you one thing it did. It cleansed me of the unrighteousness of kleptomania. Whatever tendencies I had in that direction were nipped in the bud. Never again have I taken anything from a store without paying for it. And I think that if I were ever tempted to do so, a vision of a little, white wooden chair would loom before me and stay my hand.

But in later years I have often wondered, at least for me, if confession has become too easy. The liturgical renewal which insists that a prayer of confession be included in almost every service of worship serves many useful purposes. For one thing, it recognizes that "if we say we have no sin, we deceive ourselves, and the truth is not in us." It reminds us that we are sinners saved by grace and wholly dependent upon God's grace for our forgiveness. It prods us Protestants to go through at least the motions of confession. I suspect there are some of us ("Speak for yourself, Will") who would rarely offer to God a genuine prayer of confession if we were not reminded to do so by the liturgy.

But the other side of the emphasis upon a prayer of confession, and especially a printed prayer, at every service is that it can become too routine, too general, too ritualistic, and too easy.

It seems to me that confession can become too easy when we keep on confessing to sins of which we are not guilty. Now if this seems to smack of self-righteousness, let me cite an example.

There is a prayer of confession in *The Worship Book* that has this phrase: "We walk away from neighbors in need." If we take that phrase literally and at face value we are saying that all of us walk away from our neighbors in need all the time. That simply is not true.

I know from personal experience that it is not true of this community. When I was desperately ill for several weeks last spring there was a whole host of people in this seminary family who did not walk away from this neighbor in need. You surrounded me with concern, support, practical everyday help, and prayers. Without all this I am convinced that I simply would not have made it.

It can be far too easy to say, "We walk away from neighbors in need." It seems to me to confess in such blanket terms trivializes the help and mutual concern we do have and express for each other. It tends to keep us from admitting those specific times when we do walk away from neighbors in need. I would be happier with the phrase if it said something like this: "All too often we walk away from neighbors in need," or better still, "Forgive us for those times when we do not recognize who our neighbors are and walk away from their needs."

Perhaps this sounds like nitpicking from a crotchety old cynic who has been coming to chapel too long. But if day after day I confess that I walk away from neighbors in need and time and again hear, "In Jesus Christ you are forgiven," I might decide simply to keep on walking because I am forgiven anyway. For it is easier to keep on walking than it is to take a good hard look at who my neighbors really are and how I relate to them.

It seems to me that confession is too easy when "In Jesus Christ we are forgiven" ends with a period instead of with a semicolon.

It is true that "if we confess our sins, God is faithful and just to forgive our sins," but the text completes that promise with the words "and cleanses us from all unrighteousness." It is true that Jesus Christ is our advocate who pleads our case in the courts of heaven and that he is the expiation for our sins so that we are acquitted and declared not guilty.

The same passage from 1 John calls on us to walk in the light as God is in the light. It indicates that the evidence that we are truly forgiven is that we live in the same way that Christ lived — and that, my friends, is not easy. Our failure to live up to that ideal sends us back to confession again and again. But let us be more specific about what we are confessing.

What I mean by saying that "In Jesus Christ we are forgiven" should not end in a period is that it should challenge us to ask, "Now what? Since I am forgiven, how do I respond to that great gift?"

I suppose what I am saying in theological terms is that "justification" which does not set us on the road to "sanctification" is too easy.

Mark 6:45-52

A Voice Against The Wind

Although this sermon was preached in the Columbia Chapel as late as July, 1993, it had been delivered in much the same form at numerous churches over the last several years.

It is essentially a retelling of the biblical story with the recurring refrain "against the wind" over against the I AM (ego eimi) of Jesus' voice.

The story is told in such a way as to try to draw the hearers into the emotions, sights, and sounds of the narrative so that they can identify with the sense of helplessness the disciples felt in the storm as well as the awe and assurance which swept over them when they realized that Jesus had come to them in the midst of the storm.

Most of the time the wind was their friend, the sea their home, the boat their submissive chariot. Several of these men were fishermen who drew their livelihood from the sea. With skills sharpened by long years of practice, hands and muscles hardened by constant use, they could control the boat, guide it along watery lanes, and bring it to safe and certain shores. They liked the sting of the wind in their faces, and, at times, they could capture its strength in their sails to speed them on their way.

But this time they were distressed in rowing, for the wind was against them. Their boat was on the sea in the dead of night. The darkness obscured the distant shore. The wind pushed against them like a giant hand blocking their way. All their combined skill, all their corporate muscle bent against the sturdy oars could not release them from the grip of the tossing waves which held them fast.

Not only did the boat seem to stand still except for its restless rocking, but time, too, seemed not to move. What watch of the night was it? Stars were hidden by mist and clouds; the glow of the moon could not penetrate the gloom. Darkness seemed to close in upon them. Surely dawn must come sometime, but for what seemed like days instead of hours there had been no streaks of light on any horizon.

And with the darkness, the wind, and the crashing waves there came the sense of loneliness, of near despair, of forsakenness. Twelve of them were together in the boat, but still they felt alone. The presence of the One who had made them one was not among them. He had set them on their journey in the night. He had sent them on ahead of him. Surely there was in that sending the promise of his coming, that he would meet them on the other side.

But suppose they never reached the shore. How, then, could he join them? Why had he gone up into the hills? He was there alone on the land, and they were out here on the sea in the dark, distressed in rowing, for the wind was against them.

But what they did not know, or did not have the faith to believe, was that although they could not see Jesus at prayer in the hills, he could see them on the sea, and he knew that they were distressed in rowing.

Then at last, when the night is darkest and strength is exhausted and the lamp of life burns low, in that long, lonely stretch of night just before the dawn finally breaks, in the fourth watch of the night, he came to them walking on the sea.

With what splendid restraint the story is told. Here is quiet dignity, firm assurance, unshakable authority. This is no nick-in-time rescue effort; no dashing through the waves on angel wings. But walking on the sea, like a laird striding across his acreage; like a king strolling through his realm.

In fact, Mark tells us that Jesus meant to pass them by. Did he need to come directly to them? Would it not be enough simply to show himself in silhouette, to let them know that he was near, steadfast against the wind? Would not such a passing by be enough to bolster their confidence and strengthen their faith?

Perhaps it should have been, but it was not. Such a coming did not fit their expectations nor their hopes. It shattered the limits of what they thought possible.

This was not the familiar figure whom they knew and could recognize. Jesus had startled them before by calming a storm only with his words, "Peace, be still." But that time he was in the boat with them; he had not left them alone.

But what was this strange shape striding across the waves? Who was this lordly figure defying the wind and the waves and moving majestically across the sea? Surely this was no source of comfort, but an apparition, a phantom from the realm of the dead, perhaps a sign of sure disaster.

So they cried out in terror, "It is a ghost," But the wind snatched their words and flung them scattered against the distant hills.

Then through the wind, against the wind, there came a voice, a voice which the wind could not catch nor distort: "Take heart; it is I; have no fear!"

What an extraordinary command! What a daring call for faith! "Take heart; have no fear!"

What evidence will he give to support such a call to courage? What reason will he set forth for abandoning fear?

He does not promise that the storm soon will cease. He does not say, "All will be well"; he does not declare, "Hold on a little longer; dawn is about to break"; he does not challenge: "Row harder and you will surely reach the shore."

The only word he gives them to call them to faith is this: "It is I." This word he flings against the wind. This word he brings to terrified disciples in a boat that will not move. "I AM, AND I AM HERE!"

This is a strong word. It is a revealing word. It is a word which calls for the response of faith.

When Moses stood before a burning bush and heard a command and asked the question, "Who are you?" the answer came, "I AM." This is a word which reveals that God is present and active, concerned and caring, whether spoken from a burning bush or from a voice against the wind.

After proclaiming, "Take heart; I AM; have no fear," Jesus came through the mist and got into the boat with his disciples. They were utterly astonished. His being with them still did not answer all their questions, for there was still much which they did not understand. There were lengths to go before their voyage of faith would land them on a safe and solid shore.

But the wind had ceased, the waves were calm, and the boat was on the move again, for they had heard a voice against the wind: "I AM."

Perhaps some of you have had the literal experience of being in a small craft in the dark of night, distressed in rowing because the wind was against you. If that is true, then you can identify with the disciples on the storm-tossed sea.

I have never had that experience, but I, like most of you I am sure, have known times when I was distressed in rowing because the wind was against me.

Who among us has not found himself or herself in situations which were about to overwhelm us, that were far beyond our skill or strength to control? A serious illness for ourselves or for someone whom we love; a controversy in the church which seems to have no ready resolution; tensions within the family circle which grow worse the more we try to work at them; disruptions in the world which are so deep and complex that we are at a loss to understand them, much less to know how to contribute to their salvation.

Are there not times when we dare to wonder whether God has abandoned us, whether Jesus has forgotten us, whether the Holy Spirit is after all simply a Holy Ghost?

Oh, we of little faith! Does Jesus not come to us again and again over the waves, through the darkness, with his voice against the wind?

He may not come on our terms nor according to our timetable. He may wait until the fourth watch of the night. But come he will!

Look then. That dim shape forming through the mist need not be a source of terror simply because it is new, mysterious, and does not fit what we believe is possible. Our Lord Christ exposes himself to the storm and comes to us through it.

Listen! There is a voice against the wind. The voice gives no easy assurances. But it speaks a strong word: "Take heart; have no fear, I AM." God is; God comes; God is here.

Is this not better than a smooth sea and a dull crossing?

Is this not better than a ship becalmed, rocking softly and sleepily with no shore for which to strive?

Is this not better than to feel no need for Jesus Christ to come to us in the fourth watch of the night?

Give us, then, the wind against us, the breaking waves, and a craft tossed in uncertainty and fear, if in such a setting we can see him coming to us through the dark, and hear his voice against the wind, "Take heart; have no fear; I AM!"

John 21:15-19

Isn't Once Enough?

This sermon was prepared for and preached to a seminary congregation in the chapel of Columbia Seminary in May, 1992. It was near the end of the academic year. Graduating students were taking new pastorates; many other students were going to a summer of supervised ministry or to intern years. All, in a sense, were being called to "Feed my sheep."

The sermon is a retelling of the story in John's Gospel with allusions to the stories of Jacob wrestling at the Jabbok and Peter's denial of Jesus. The hope is that the hearers will identify with Peter's struggle as he responds to Jesus' repeated question, "Do you love me?"

The conclusion is a kind of personal confession showing that the preacher identifies both with Peter's struggle to respond to Jesus as well as with that of the hearers.

"Simon, son of John; Simon, son of John; Simon, son of John."

Peter could hardly reply with naive surprise. "Oh, were you talking to me?"

"Do you love me; do you love me; do you love me?"

Like a sleepy student in a 2:00 class, Peter could hardly mumble, "Sorry, but I did not quite get the question. Would you mind repeating it?"

"Feed my lambs; tend my sheep; feed my sheep."

Peter could hardly take refuge in literalism and object. "But I'm no shepherd. I'm a fisherman by trade."

Three times three for Peter. Isn't once enough?

By that three times three repetition of name, question, and task, Peter is surrounded, hedged about, encountered by the probing, specific words of Jesus Christ. Peter may wish to play the artful dodger, but there are no back alleys for him to slip into and make his escape. If he turns one way the sound of his name pursues him. If he takes a step or two to the side the question echoes and re-echoes in his ears. If he makes an about-face — Feed. Tend. Feed — will not let him go.

It reminds me a little of Jacob wrestling at the Jabbok. Here is the muscular, persistent Jesus who will not let Peter go, not even at the break of day.

Surely Peter feels that once is enough. The text says, "Peter was grieved because he said to him the *third* time...." Once is understandable. Twice could be for emphasis. But three times?

The setting and the three times three, do these stir Peter's memory?

There is a charcoal fire on the beach. Peter and the others stand by the fire and warm themselves and dry out after a night of fishing. The firelight plays on Peter's rugged features. The flames seem to dance in the depths of Jesus' eyes.

Does Peter remember another charcoal fire at which he warmed himself? Does Peter remember that at that fire, too, there was a question directed to him and that the question was repeated three times? "Are you not one of this man's disciples?"

To that question Peter answered unhesitatingly, without qualification, "I am not."

As he stood and warmed himself at that other fire Peter denied his own identity — "I AM NOT A DISCIPLE." Now as this morning fire is dying out Jesus is calling his name. "Simon, son of John."

As he stood and warmed himself at that other fire Peter disclaimed his love and loyalty to Jesus. He denied that he had ever been with Jesus or even knew him. Now beside the ashy embers of a new fire Jesus asks him, "Do you love me?"

To answer the question, "Do you love me?" does not come easily for Peter. To say baldly and boldly, "I love you," without some evidence to back it up seems presumptuous. But Peter is beyond seeking to parade blustery proof. Too many times in the past he had gotten his feet tangled in his awkward efforts to prove his love and loyalty.

On the night of Jesus' arrest Peter had struck a mighty blow for righteousness and succeeded in cutting off the ear of the servant of the High Priest. Hardly a decisive victory. Jesus had responded, "Put your sword in its sheath."

At one time Peter had said to Jesus, "I will lay down my life for you," but had quailed and wept at the crowing of the cock at dawn.

This time Peter seeks to make no self-righteous claims, to offer no proof. Instead of seeking to bolster his "I love you" with evidence of his own, he rests his case upon what Jesus knows to be in his heart. "Lord, you know — you know everything; you know that I love you."

But if Jesus knows and Peter knows that he knows, then why is Jesus so persistent with the question? Is he raising doubts about Peter's loyalty? Is he trying to taunt Peter into adding adjectives, underlining the verb, and making a list of reasons?

Surely none of these! Is it not rather a gracious persistence? True, it touches the exposed, tender nerve of Peter's memory, but does it not give opportunity for healing? Do three questions and three answers — "Are you?" — "I am not" — still weigh heavily on Peter's mind? What better way to let them fade than to overshadow them with three positive answers, the chance to confess with sincerity but without swagger, "Yes, Lord, I love you ..."?

That Jesus knows that Peter speaks the truth is shown by his response, "Feed my sheep." For only one who loves the good shepherd can be trusted to tend his flock. Peter needs to understand that love is not a private matter between himself and Jesus. He needs to know that the profession is not complete when the correct words are spoken. The correct answer inevitably carries with it a commitment which Jesus makes plain and specific, "Feed my sheep."

Green pastures — still waters — the safety of the fold? Yes, sometimes. That is part of tending the sheep. But there is also the constant vigilance; the dogged faithfulness; the far pastures beyond the world; the dangers from the thief and the wolf. There is keeping on until one is bound and carried where one does not wish to go. Peter will fulfill his earlier promise, "I will lay down my life for you."

131

You see. The persistent Christ will not let Peter go — not even at the break of day. He binds him to himself even to death and beyond. For since it is the crucified risen Christ who says to Peter, "Follow me," that must mean to follow beyond the dawn into a new and glorious day.

I have the feeling that Peter in this story was not entirely comfortable with this persistent Christ. Nor am I sure that I am comfortable with him now.

I think I like it better when my name is not called quite so often or so specifically. I like it better when I can be a member of Christians anonymous, when I can sort of fade into the comfortableness of the corporate and be a kind of Christian in general where I don't feel any particular, sharp, individual responsibilities.

I think I would like it better if he would be satisfied with my saying once and for all, "Yes, Lord ..." and let it go at that. For if he keeps on asking the question, if he keeps on challenging me to declare my faith, then I have to ponder the implications of what I mean by my "Yes," and that makes me vulnerable.

And do I have to be reminded constantly of those blessed sheep? If he keeps on urging me to tend them and feed them then I can hardly forget that there are other sheep beyond this fold for whom I should seek; that there are those who are literally hungry whom I am supposed to feed.

Really, Lord, couldn't you let up just a little? Isn't once enough?

But while I may not be entirely comfortable with this muscular, persistent Christ — like Jacob at the Jabbok, I do not want to let him go, nor do I want him to relax his grip on me.

For if he keeps calling my name then he knows that I am here. He has not forgotten me nor given up on me. He knows who I am. I am not a faceless member of the multitude. I am — ungrammatically — *ME*!

If he keeps asking, "Do you love me?" then it matters to him whether I do or not, or he would not ask the question so often.

And if he accepts my repeated answer, "Yes, Lord, you know ..." that means that he accepts the incomplete love which he knows that I have for him.

If he keeps reminding me of those sheep and that I am to be a shepherd to them then he has given me his own task to do in the world. He has more faith and confidence in me than I have in myself. He trusts me.

I don't know about you, but I am grateful for this persistent Christ who will not let me go. For my memory is too short and my zeal too easily cooled for once to be enough.

For me it takes three times three — and more.

What about you?

When The Wine Fails

This homily was prepared for and preached at the wedding in Norfolk, Virginia, of Kathryn Johnson and David Cameron, both ordained Presbyterian ministers.

There is an imaginary retelling of the biblical story suggesting why the wine failed and how Jesus intervened in the situation.

A parallel is suggested between the joy of the wedding in Cana and the present one in Norfolk. The failure of the wine is taken as looking to the future with a sense of the reality of relationships. The high romance of the wedding day is not likely to last for the long haul. But if there is a commitment to Jesus Christ on the part of bride and groom they may discover in later years that their joy and love is deeper and stronger than it was at the beginning. They may well find that they have saved the best wine until last.

Of course, I do not know why the wine ran out at the marriage feast at Cana in Galilee, but I can hazard a guess.

Do you suppose that when they were planning that wedding all the principals said to each other, "Now, we are going to keep this simple. We aren't going to plan anything too elaborate, and we are going to keep the guest list to the wedding feast down to a manageable size — just family and the very closest friends."

But inevitably as the time drew nearer things began to get out of hand a little. The guest list which was going to be kept small with strict and ruthless discipline began to grow.

Perhaps the groom's mother said, "You know, I really would like for you to invite Mary of Nazareth. She and I have been such good friends since we ..."

135

"Well, yes," the groom replied. "I think it would be nice for her to come. I'd like to have her here. I remember how she used to bring me fig cakes when I was a kid."

Then another relative spoke up and said, "Yes, but to invite Mary does present another problem. We can hardly invite her without asking her son, Jesus. After all, he has been making something of a name for himself lately. If we invited Mary and did not invite her son it might look as if we were deliberately slighting him."

And another said, "But you know he hardly ever goes anywhere alone. He has a bunch of disciples who seem to follow him everywhere. If we invite Jesus I'm sure his disciples will come, too. And we have no idea how many of them there might be."

So the guest list grew, and the plans for the wedding feast were expanded. It was a festive and joyous occasion, as most weddings are and should be. A high moment of excitement, a time of intense anticipation. The marking of a new beginning for two lives joined in love and commitment.

Therefore, celebration was appropriate, and the providers of the feast did all they could to make it a time of joy, of conviviality, of laughter, of lighthearted happiness. Among other things they provided wine, good wine — and surely in abundance enough for any reasonable use.

But what with all the extra guests and some miscalculations about how thirsty the crowd would be, the wine failed before the celebration was over. The supply ran out. In spite of all their careful planning, their resources were not enough for the occasion. When the wine failed the feast was in danger of dampening down into a subdued and grumbling gathering from which dissatisfied guests would begin to drift away, leaving an embarrassed and questioning couple.

But at this marriage feast there was a particular guest. He may have been among those who we have imagined swelled the guest list beyond the expected. At any rate, his presence proved to make a surprising and mysterious difference when the wine failed.

The gathered company had not yet become aware of the crisis. But his insightful and concerned mother called his attention to it. He did not disrupt the festivities to reassure the guests — or the host — not to worry, that everything would be all right. He did not announce that he was about to perform a miracle. With quiet authority he gave a few orders. Six stone jars, each holding at least twenty gallons, were filled with water — plain, clear, ordinary water. From one of the jars a chalice was filled and taken to the steward of the feast. The steward tasted the cup with delightful surprise. His face lit up with wonder.

I suspect that the bridegroom was not a little puzzled when the laughing steward clapped him on the shoulder and said, "You rascal! You wait until all have drunk their fill — and then you bring out this incredibly invigorating wine. You have kept the good wine until now."

And the steward and the bridegroom both would have been aghast if they had known that there still were about 120 gallons of that rare vintage left over. I wonder if the guests found out that all those tall stone jars were full of wine better than they had ever tasted before. If they did find out, I wonder how long that marriage feast lasted.

We tend to think of this familiar story of the marriage feast when the wine failed and a miracle took place as a unique and unusual event — and indeed it was. For the Gospel of John is at pains to make it plain that in this story Jesus Christ manifested his glory, and that it was a basis of faith and belief for his disciples. In some way, then, the very glory of God was revealed at the marriage feast at Cana in the person and deed of Jesus.

But in another sense, this story reflects what happens — or can happen — with marriages.

The wedding day is a time well planned, meticulously prepared for, abundantly provided for to assure a perfect day, a day that is image of, prelude to, and preparation for a perfect blending of two lives for an indefinite and unruffled future.

The expected wine provided by the host is symbol of the happiness, the high hopes, the excitement, the exhilaration of this particular, special day. But inevitably that wine fails. The immediate supply of exquisite joy diminishes. It begins to fade as life settles back into routine and regularity; as the bride and groom take up again their daily tasks, add some responsibilities to those already theirs, and find that marriage has not removed all the drudgery and frustration from daily toil; as they discover foibles, peculiarities, irritations in each other that had remained well hidden or cleverly disguised, or which they had failed to see with prenuptial starry eyes. There is always the possibility that the wedding feast will come to an end before its time.

But a miracle can happen if that marriage has been made in the presence of and with openness to the transforming power of Jesus Christ. Quite surprisingly he can take the overabundance of ordinary, routine days and make them better and more invigorating than any marriage feast has ever been. Quietly, without sounding a trumpet before him, Jesus turned plain, ordinary water into an abundance of the very best wine. Trust him, then, to transform all those ordinary tomorrows into the very best of times.

One way the glory is manifested in Jesus Christ is that he comes into and shares with us the significant moments of our lives, such as being a guest at a marriage at Cana in Galilee — or in Norfolk in Virginia. But even more remarkable is that he is God with us in the long haul, in the ongoingness of human existence, and that he is there to make all things new when the wine fails.

I am sure that Kathryn and David will forever cherish the memories of this joyful day, and that they are grateful for all that has been done to make it so. But because they have committed their lives not only to each other but also to Jesus Christ, let them look ahead with confidence to many a day in the future which could hardly be called remarkable — except for this: that at the close of some of those days they will look at each other, perhaps take each other by the hand as they soon will do in this ceremony, and with a mischievous twinkle in their eyes and the lilt of surprise and gratitude in their voices say to each other, "You have kept the best wine until now."

Three Loaves At Midnight

This sermon was prepared for and preached at a chapel service at Columbia Seminary at which the Lord's Supper was celebrated. The bread was three loaves in a basket on the Table. These loaves were broken at the time of the distribution of the elements. The Moores referred to lived next door to me at the time. Mrs. Moore was manager of the seminary dining hall.

The sermon is essentially a retelling of the biblical passage with the use of some imagination. The conclusion applies the eucharistic motifs of the parable to the Lord's Supper and to the practice of ministry. The sermon departs from the usual interpretation which has the man making the request knocking loudly on the door and the man inside answering reluctantly. This interpretation owes a great deal to Kenneth E. Bailey's exegesis of the Parable in Poet and Peasant Through Peasant Eyes, *pp. 119-141.*

What a complicated network of relationships clusters around those three loaves at midnight.

There is the weary traveler after we know not how long a journey seeking hospitality at his friend's house. It is late, but he knows full well that he will be received because in that culture hospitality is mandatory, and the one whose house he seeks is his friend.

But his arrival must be unexpected, for his friend is not prepared for guests. Oh, the friend does not hesitate to receive the guest, but what will he set before him to let him know that he is truly welcomed? There are no fresh baked loaves in the house, for this household's baking day is yet a day away. There are broken fragments left over from the family meal eaten just after sunset. But these will not do for a guest. What to do when the host wishes to spread a bountiful table but has only ordinary fare, and not enough of that?

Midnight it may be, but the friend who is the host knows where there is bread enough and to spare — the house two doors down the street. Today he saw the woman of the house coming from the village ovens, her basket brimming with fresh baked bread. He can still smell the warm aroma of the yeasty loaves.

There he will go and ask. He will not ask for everything. He will ask for only three loaves, more than enough for his guest, enough to symbolize welcome, but little enough so that his neighbor can easily spare it.

The host invites his traveling friend to make himself comfortable and then slips out into the darkened street to the house two doors down. He puts his lips close to the chink in the door and calls out in a voice loud enough to be heard within, but not raucous enough to arouse the neighbors, for, after all, it is midnight.

"Friend, lend me three loaves, for a friend of mine has arrived on a journey and I have nothing to set before him."

The householder inside stirs in his bed. "Friend, lend me three loaves ..." echoes in his ear. Is he dreaming or is someone outside asking for three loaves? He sits up in bed. The voice sounds familiar.

"Eleazar, is that you?" he asks in a stage whisper.

"Yes, Ezekiel, it is I. Please, lend me three loaves for a friend of mine...."

"I heard you the first time. Keep your voice down. You will wake the children, and what is worse, you will wake my wife."

Ezekiel sits there in the night and thinks of all the excuses he could give.

"It's midnight, man, and the door is shut. It is too much trouble to get up and open it. We just got these kids settled down, and one of them is already beginning to whimper a little. Go somewhere else to borrow bread."

But Ezekiel knows that he could never give these excuses. He might if the three loaves at midnight were a matter only between himself and Eleazar. But what would the traveler think if he came to this village and his host had a difficult time giving him a decent meal? What kind of neighbors would he think Eleazar had if he could not borrow as little as three loaves? And what would the whole town say the next day when they found out that a friend had asked for bread to set before a guest and had been refused?

In those three loaves at midnight Ezekiel's whole sense of honor and integrity is at stake. Midnight or not, shut door or not, sleeping kids or not, he must be true to himself and to his community. So he gets up quickly, gathers not only the three loaves but whatever else is needed for a welcoming meal. He puts it all in a big basket, takes it to the door, opens the door, and gives it to Eleazar.

Eleazar hurries back to his own home and his weary, traveling friend. He spreads a white linen cloth on the table. From the basket he takes out all the things Ezekiel has given him. He lays before his friend a feast, with the three loaves in the center of the table.

The three loaves at midnight have done their work.

The traveler is properly welcomed. He eats, is satisfied, is strengthened for his further journey, and his weariness is relieved.

The host has extended proper hospitality. He has become host indeed. Although his own resources had not been enough, he did not hesitate to seek the place of bread, to ask for three loaves, and to trust that he would receive them in the middle of the night.

The householder who had the bread can shut his door again, lie down surrounded by his sleeping children, and know that he has been true to himself and has not betrayed the honor of his village.

There are three loaves on the Table before us. Where did they come from? If we want to be literal about it, they came from Sedera Moore in the dining hall. Let me assure you that I did not obtain them by going next door to the Moores' house at midnight and calling out, "Friend, lend me three loaves." However, there have been times enough when I have disturbed the Moores' midnight rest in some crisis situation and have never been refused.

But if we put these loaves in the context of the words of Jesus and the atmosphere of the Lord's Supper, they come from God. For the parable is preceded by Jesus' teaching his disciples to pray, "Father ... give us this day our daily bread." Thus does Jesus recognize God as the one who supplies our needs, the basic, daily, on-going needs symbolized by bread. By giving us the prayer he encourages us to ask for bread and to expect to receive it.

141

The parable is followed by a series of sayings in which Jesus assures us that God is far more abundantly generous than any earthly friend or parent. He gives far more than bread. He gives himself.

But what has the parable to suggest about the three loaves on the Table? Perhaps it has a special word to say to those of us who as ministers seek to play the role of host.

How often the weary traveler comes — some crisis situation, unexpected, unprepared for, at some inconvenient hour. We wish to welcome and receive the traveler; we want to handle the situation in the most appropriate, best way possible. But of ourselves we have nothing to set before the guest, and we know it.

All our accepting, pastoral skills somehow do not work. All our careful analysis of the biblical text falls flat. All our carefully crafted proclamations of the good news seem as only clanging cymbals. All our quoting of learned theologians sounds hollow.

None of these put forward as our own skill, achievement, accomplishment take the place of bread.

But we need not despair. Go out into the darkness to the House of Bread. For if we know anything or believe anything it is that we know where there is bread enough and to spare. We know where the supply is fresh every morning and new every evening and where midnight itself is no deterrent.

Be bold to ask, and expect to receive. If a sleepy villager will answer readily and abundantly the request of a desperate friend, how much more will God, true to his character, supply whatever we need?

We who serve in ministry and who thus serve at this Table are not the suppliers of the bread, nor are we the hosts. We only receive, offer, and distribute that which Another provides.

Jesus Christ is both Host and Feast. He invites us all to come. He supplies the midnight meal. What he offers is his body broken, his blood shed, for us.

Surely in this bread and cup we can have our hunger satisfied, our weariness relieved, our strength renewed for the further journey.

Be assured that the One who hears our cry for three loaves at midnight will rise and give us whatever we need.

See! He already has, for the loaves are on the Table.

Barefoot In The Pulpit

This sermon was prepared especially for a congregation of ministers. It was used, in slightly different forms, at a ministers' conference, in the chapel of Columbia Seminary, and at several ordination/installation services for young ministers. At one such service the young man who was being installed came forward to answer the required questions after he had removed his shoes.

The sermon combines personal experience with the story of Moses and the burning bush. It seeks to draw parallels between Moses' experience of standing on holy ground with that of the minister who has responded to God's call, and, as a result, stands in the pulpit regularly.

I have a kind of obsession about the shoes I wear in the pulpit. I would not dare enter the pulpit in shoes of any color except black. Why am I so strict about wearing only black shoes in the pulpit? It is because when I was a student at Columbia Seminary over half a century ago, Dr. J. McDowell Richards was president of the seminary. He drilled it into our heads, or at least into my head, that the only appropriate color shoes to be worn in the pulpit is black. Therefore, for me to wear some other color shoes in the pulpit would be a form of heresy and a desecration of the memory of Dr. Richards.

A few years ago I went up into the mountains of North Carolina to baptize infant twins of friends of mine. When I arrived on Friday afternoon I found that I had forgotten to pack my black shoes. All I had were the shoes I wore up there — caramel-colored loafers.

All day long on Saturday I wrestled in agony about how I could get hold of some black shoes. No one in the gathered company had black shoes that would fit me. The little town did not boast a shoe store. Finally in late afternoon a friend and I drove over winding mountain roads to a town about ten miles away where there was a nice department store. There, by the providence of God, I found a pair of black shoes on sale for $25.

They fit me. I bought them. In proper ecclesiastical garb I baptized the babies. That was five years ago. I still have that pair of black shoes, and I wear them every Sunday. I have them on right now.

But you know, I did have another alternative which I did not think of at the time. Instead of going through so much trouble to get black shoes I could have worn no shoes at all. I could have come into the pulpit wearing robe and stole, but absolutely barefoot. Now the family of the baptized babies probably would have been shocked; the congregation doubtless would have been puzzled to say the least; there might have been a ripple of not very well suppressed snickers in the sanctuary.

But God might have been pleased. I think God would have smiled, not from amusement, but from delight. I think God would have been pleased if he knew that I came barefoot into the pulpit, not because I could not find any black shoes, but because I remembered Moses, and a bush that flared and flamed with swirling fire but was not consumed; if he thought I, too, had heard God's voice calling my name and saying to me, "Put off your shoes from your feet, for the place on which you are standing is holy ground."

Surely for Moses the place on which he stood looked no different from the rest of the land over which he had led the family sheep. True, it was illuminated by the flames of the burning bush. But that was not what made it holy.

For Moses the burning bush was a puzzlement, a curiosity, something to turn aside to see. Did you notice in the text that when the voice spoke out of the bush and called Moses by name, that Moses expressed no wonder or surprise? He simply answered, "Here am I."

It was not until he realized to whom the voice belonged that he hid his face and was afraid. It must have been at that point that he took off his shoes and stood on the sandy ground exposed,

144

unprotected, vulnerable. The soles of his bare feet were in direct contact with the holy ground. I wonder if he did not feel some tingling of energy, some surge of power as he wiggled his toes in the sand.

Moses knew the ground was holy when he realized that at this place he was in the presence of God and that God was communicating with him; God was revealing himself to Moses.

"I am the God of your father...." This was no new God. This was the God of all history, the God of Moses' heritage, the God of all the generations on earth. "The God of Abraham, the God of Isaac, the God of Jacob...."

He was a God involved, intertwined, concerned for the realities of human existence. Listen to the good news he brought to Moses: "I have seen ... I have heard ... I know ... I have come...." Here is a God whose majesty and might are symbolized by leaping flames of fire, flames which preserve rather than destroy the living bush. But here is a God with a compassionate human face. "I have seen the misery of my people; I have heard their cry; I know their suffering."

But once this God sees, hears, and knows, he acts. "I have come down to deliver them."

Good news for Moses. The Lord does care about the slavery, oppression, and injustice which Moses' kinfolks are enduring back in Egypt. And God himself is going to do something about it. No doubt Moses, too, had been anxious about the situation. I can imagine that he had tossed in his bedroom at night while he kept watch over his family's sheep. But what could he do about it? He had struck one blow for their freedom, and his own people had rejected his efforts. Now he was only a shepherd working for somebody else, working for his father-in-law at that.

But this God is full of surprises. He got Moses' attention with a burning bush. He scared him half to death by telling him to take his shoes off and stand on holy ground. Then he gave Moses the shock of his life by announcing that this business of liberating God's people was going to be a joint venture between Moses and God.

"So come, I will send you to Pharaoh to bring my people, the Israelites, out of Egypt."

If I had been Moses I think this would be the time to reach down and start putting on my shoes. I would have been ready to make tracks away from the holy ground, away from the burning bush, away from the revealing Voice.

But Moses, barefoot, stood his holy ground and contended with God for a while. He blurted out a natural and understandable question: "Who am I that I should go to Pharaoh, and bring the Israelites out of Egypt?"

The Lord did not answer Moses by listing all Moses' qualifications for the job. God answered him with a two-pronged promise. The first part of the promise was: "I will be with you."

Moses would find his identity and authority in his relationship to God. Moses was the "God-with-me" person. The way would be hard; the obstacles, fierce; the difficulties, seemingly insurmountable. But Moses could always remember God's words: "I will be with you."

The second part of the promise was: "When you have brought the people out of Egypt, you shall worship God on this mountain." The task, with God's help, would be accomplished. Moses would lead out a worshiping people, a people who acknowledged God as the one who gave them their identity.

But Moses went still further in his encounter with God. He wanted to know God's name. The people would surely say to Moses, "You claim that God sent you. Who is this God? Does he have a name?"

God's answer was mysterious, enigmatic, and profound: "I am who I am. Tell them I AM has sent you."

What more was there to say? What further authority did Moses need? The One who is pure existence had sent him; the source and sustainer of all there is in the universe was calling him to a task.

Are there ways in which our ministries reflect some of the luster of the ministry of Moses?

Did it not begin with some mysterious vision; perhaps not a burning bush, but a kindling stirring within the spirit? Was there not a time when we heard a Voice calling our name?

Have we not encountered a God who sees, who hears, who knows, who comes down to deliver his people? Is this not the good

146

news we have received and in which we stand? Is not the human face of God the face of Jesus Christ?

Have we not heard that chilling but thrilling word spoken directly to us, "I will send you"?

Who among us has not answered, "But, Lord, who am I to take your freeing word to the people?"

The answer keeps coming, "I will be with you." So we keep on going despite "the relentless return of the Sabbath," despite too few hours in the day, despite our own imperfections and those of our people.

Does the routine regularity of standing in the pulpit tempt us to see that place as ordinary ground?

I challenge you some day to be audacious enough to stand barefoot in the pulpit and to tell your people why you are wearing no shoes.

John 21:1-14

A New Day Begins With Breakfast

This sermon was preached at a regular worship service in the chapel of Columbia Seminary. It was during the last few days of the academic year. Doubtless many in the congregation were weary of the routine and pressures of academic life. The sermon was an attempt to remind us all that Jesus Christ can reveal himself in the everyday activities of life as well as in the more spectacular events of our spiritual journey.

The sermon begins with a personal experience and then moves into a retelling of the biblical story which suggests the feelings and emotions of the disciples during their experience of having breakfast with Jesus after a night of fruitless fishing and the transforming power of an act of revelation by the Risen Christ.

I truly believe that a new day begins with breakfast. A few years ago a cousin of mine was coming to Atlanta for a rather extended business trip. She wrote and asked if she could stay at my house while she was here. In order to show how little trouble she would be she said, "I will leave early in the morning, and I won't come home until late afternoon — and I don't eat breakfast. If you see any problem with my staying at your house don't hesitate to say so."

I wrote her back: "I see only one problem with your staying at my house. I do not approve of people who don't eat breakfast. If you stay at my house, you will eat breakfast."

She came. She ate breakfast. I saw her recently, and she told me that she still eats breakfast. So I count her a convert to the theological doctrine that a new day begins with breakfast.

Some of you are probably somewhat skeptical about my raising the statement, "A new day begins with breakfast," to the status of a theological doctrine, but I hope to justify it based on the passage of scripture I just read from John's Gospel.

What a strange resurrection appearance story this is — frustrated fishermen, a miraculous catch, and breakfast by the sea.

Wouldn't it be better if the Gospel of John ended with the dramatic scene of the crucified, risen Christ confronting the skeptical Thomas and inviting him to touch the wounds in his hands and his side? Doesn't the Gospel reach its climax with the high confession of Thomas, "My Lord and my God"? Isn't this story of a fruitless night of fishing a letdown, an anticlimax?

But in spite of all the theories about why the twenty-first chapter of John seems to be tacked on at the end and out of place, perhaps it is exactly where it ought to be. It adds an element of down-to-earth reality in how to deal with the mystery of the resurrection in everyday life. Who among us could sing — or listen to — "The Hallelujah Chorus" every day?

Some days after the first Easter, Peter announces, "I am going fishing." There is a quick response from six other of the disciples, "We will go with you."

The first excitement of the empty tomb, the thrilling wonder of the sudden appearances must have levelled off. The disciples must have begun to say to themselves, "Now what?" Peter's blunt announcement, "I am going fishing," is welcomed relief. They are glad for some specific suggestion for positive action.

Fishing was what most of these seven knew best. It was part of their daily lives, or had been before they gave it up to follow Jesus of Nazareth around Galilee and finally to Jerusalem. It would be good to feel the buoyancy of the sea under them again, to know the sting of the spray on their faces, to feel the tug of the burdened nets. To share the comradeship of hard physical toil. Then, too, life has to go on, miracle or no miracle.

But for these seven fishermen the old routine has lost something of its zest. Back to the good old days does not quite work out. They fish all night with all the combined skill they can muster, but it comes to nothing. They cast the nets as deftly as ever; they pull them in with the same smooth rhythm they always use. But they come up slack and limp. Empty and dripping. The night wears on. The morning begins to come, and wearily they make for the shore. What a discouraging voyage for the seven. If they cannot take up where they left off before their interlude with Jesus, then what to do? If after the high excitement of resurrection day life simply settles back, not only into routine and mediocrity, but also into failure and pointlessness, what is there to hope for? What are they supposed to do now?

Well, they could go on to the shore and start the day with breakfast....

And that is exactly what happens.

The morning begins for them as many a morning in the past. The night of fishing over, the boat pulling for the shore, someone on the beach in the early light — a customer perhaps looking for the freshest catch — calling out the time-honored question put to fishermen, "Have you caught anything?" Their dispirited answer: "Nothing."

There must have been many a morning in the past when they built a fire on the beach, laid bread and fresh fish on the glowing coals, and had breakfast by the sea.

But this time these two everyday, routine fisherman experiences are set forth in scripture as revelations of the reality of the resurrection of Jesus Christ. See how the story begins: "After this Jesus revealed himself again to the disciples by the sea of Tiberias; and he revealed himself in this way...." Listen how the story ends: "This was now the third time Jesus was revealed to the disciples after he was raised from the dead."

Is this the way the risen Christ makes himself known, by asking empty-handed fishermen, "Have you caught anything?"; by sharing breakfast by the sea at the beginning of the day? From this story it seems so.

But there is a new dimension to this particular morning. The man on the beach is not content with the disconsolate answer: "Nothing." He takes charge of the situation, speaks an authoritative word, and things begin to happen and to change.

"Cast the net on the right side of the boat, and you will find some." They obey his word. Where before the net had been limp and empty, the fishermen discouraged, there is now an overabundance of fish, excited fishermen splashing to shore, the joy and abandon of life having meaning again as they drag the bulging nets to land.

And the breakfast by the sea. The menu is no different from a thousand times before, but this time the atmosphere is transformed. They know themselves to be in the presence of the risen Lord. They do not argue among themselves about who he is. There is a mysterious certainty that the one who prepares and shares breakfast with them is Jesus Christ, crucified, risen, alive, Lord.

So you see, if Easter is really true, if it is more than an annual rite of spring, if Jesus Christ indeed is raised, then a new day does not have to begin with a blast of trumpets, or the roll of supernal drums, or the soaring anthems of a heavenly choir. A new day can begin with breakfast. The most routine and ordinary meal of the day.

It is a way of saying that the risen Christ often comes to us in the ordinary daily routine of our lives; that he can speak an authoritative word which challenges us to action and restores meaning and purpose to our being; that the resurrection transforms not only the sweep of history, but also the ongoing human existence of this present life.

In the light of the resurrection a new day begins with breakfast because every day is new. Every day is resurrection day.

Now do you understand why, if you stay at my house, you are going to eat breakfast?

Advent On A Shoestring

This sermon was first preached in the chapel of Columbia Seminary during the Advent season of 1987. It has been used since that time in two churches during Advent.

It uses the image of untying shoestrings based on John the Baptist's declaration that he was not worthy to untie the thongs of Jesus' sandals. Then it lays alongside that story the narrative of Jesus washing the disciples' feet. The one whose shoes John did not feel worthy to untie, removes the shoes of his disciples and washes their feet.

By considering these two stories from the Gospel of John the sermon seeks to combine both the divine exaltation and the gracious humility of the Incarnation which is celebrated at Advent. It also makes use of a brief "visual aid" at the conclusion.

Shoestrings are not very glamorous articles of clothing. Some shoes, thankfully, do not require them. I prefer shoes which slip on rather than those which tie on. Shoestrings can be troublesome. Those of you who wear them have probably had the experience of having one break at the most crucial and inappropriate moment.

I remember some years ago traveling to a distant city to make a speech at a special Wednesday night dinner in a particular church. I flew, but the schedule to that city required that I change planes twice. Every plane that I boarded that day was delayed for some reason or other. So instead of arriving in early afternoon in time for a leisurely rest — and to finish writing my speech — I landed a scant hour before the dinner was to begin. I was whisked off to the place where I was to stay, took a quick shower to wash off the grime of all-day travel, and dressed hurriedly. As I bent down to tie my shoes I tugged at one of the strings. It broke and I lifted a dangling stub in my hand. I must admit that my ministerial language was sorely tried on that occasion.

Shoestrings are also troublesome because it is difficult to tie or untie them without getting into a rather awkward and undignified position. One either has to put one foot on the other knee, or bend over and try to reach one's feet on the floor — an accomplishment which becomes increasingly difficult with advancing age.

And if one has occasion to tie or untie the shoes of another it can hardly be done without stooping down or kneeling before the one whose shoes need attention.

"There was a man sent from God whose name was John." Now surely one sent from God could go around tying or untying the shoes of anyone he chose. Or what is more likely one sent from God would hardly consider the menial task of untying another's shoes an act consistent with or worthy of divine commission. Does God, the sovereign of the universe, send ambassadors into this world to contend with shoestrings? What interest could God have in such insignificant, mundane, humble strands of thread?

And yet John, the man sent from God, when he wanted to express the awe and wonder and magnificence of his mission, talked about shoestrings; he talked about not being worthy to untie the thongs of another's sandals.

How worthy does one have to be to untie a shoestring? To do so hardly ranks with placing a crown on another's head, or pinning a medal on another's uniform, or draping a doctor's hood over another's shoulders. You have to be somebody; you must have status; you need authoritative rank to do any of those things. But could not just about anybody off the street untie a shoestring — the lowliest servant, the most ignorant, unskilled beggar? It would seem so.

And yet John said, "One comes after me the thong of whose sandal I am not worthy to untie."

John felt himself unworthy not because his hands were unclean, not because he was a notorious sinner — for he was neither of these. He felt unworthy because of the status, the character, the mission of the one who wore the sandals.

John had been sent from God to prepare the way for another. "Make straight the way of the Lord," he declared. His mission was to proclaim, "Behold, the Lamb of God who takes away the sin of the world ... This is He who baptizes with the Holy Spirit ... This is the Son of God."

John made it clear that he was not to be confused either by himself or by others with the one who came after him. It was one thing to be sent from God. It was quite another thing to be God Incarnate in the flesh.

Can you imagine God in shoes, striding the golden streets of Heaven, leaping from star to star and leaving footprints on the planets along the silvery pavement of the Milky Way?

But John was convinced that the full expression of God — God's Word — did indeed wear sandals and walk the grimy roads of Earth. John would do all he could to smooth the roads and level the paths for those sandaled feet — but to come so close, to be so familiar, as to stoop down, reach out, touch those feet and untie the thong of those sandals ... Who dares touch the shoestrings of God?

The thongs of Jesus' sandals call to mind the paradox of the awe, the mystery, the wonder of Advent. Who is it for whom we wait? Who is it who comes? "The Word was made flesh and dwelt among us, full of grace and truth; we have beheld his glory, glory as of the only Son of the Father." And yet that word, that glory, comes wearing sandals with thongs to be untied — but who can be found worthy to untie them?

Then are we not caught in a dilemma? If we dare not approach near enough to touch his feet; if we must always kneel before him with eyes averted and cast down; if we are forever to draw back from the most menial task for him because we are unworthy — then how are we to come to know him; how are we to walk the road with him; how are we to serve him; how are we to recognize that our flesh is his flesh?

The wonder of Advent grows and deepens when we get a glimpse of another scene where shoestrings need to be untied.

The scene is introduced by phrases which have the arresting resonance of supernal trumpets. One could take them to be the opening notes of the overture to creation, or the prelude to the

155

Ascension. Listen to their majesty: "Jesus knew that his hour had come to depart out of this world to the Father. He knew that the Father had given all things into his hands, and that he had come from God and was going to God."

But what does Jesus do in that cosmic hour? How does he respond to the realization of his close identity with God? How does he express the divine authority which God has given into his hands?

He rises from his place at table; he kneels before each of his disciples; he unties their shoes.

Oh, yes. I know that historically and culturally it is more precise to say that doubtless the disciples' shoes had already been removed when they reclined at table. But symbolically Jesus looses their shoestrings and removes their sandals — for feet must be made bare if they are to be washed.

He takes their feet in his hands. He washes away the dirt and grime of the road. He cools them with the fresh water from the basin. He gently rubs their calluses. He refreshes and relaxes their feet as he vigorously dries them with the coarse towel knotted around his waist. And he does all this without forgetting or letting them forget who he is or who they are.

Advent on a shoestring is the magnificent mixture of the exaltation and the humility of God in Jesus Christ. The one the thongs of whose sandals we are not worthy to untie comes to us, unties our shoes, slips off our shoes, and washes our weary feet. And we are ready for the road again. The reason he comes to us wearing shoes is so that he can walk the same roads we walk.

Are we aware at this Advent season of those about us who are weary of the road, whose feet are hot and sore, the thongs of whose sandals are too tightly bound? Do we draw back from stooping down and untying their shoestrings not because we feel unworthy to do so, but because we fear that they do not deserve our service?

Thank God the One who stoops down at Advent to loose the thongs of our sandals is not deterred because we are unworthy.

Hear his haunting words. "If I, your Lord and Teacher, have washed your feet, you also ought to wash one another's feet. For I have given you an example, that you also should do as I have done to you."

You know, when I go home today I think I will drape a shoe-string on one branch of my Christmas tree.

(While saying the last sentence I held up a shoestring draped over both hands. Several people told me as they left the service, "I think I will put a shoestring on my Christmas tree, too.")

Philippians 1:1-21

On Being Thankful On Cue

This sermon is clearly "historically conditioned." It was preached to a seminary congregation in the chapel of Columbia Seminary on the last day of classes before the Thanksgiving holidays. The year was 1986, and many of the historical allusions reflect the events and mood of that time.

There is generous use of the first-person singular pronoun. This is done to avoid the accusatory stance of berating the hearers for their possible lack of gratitude at the Thanksgiving season. It also is designed to expose the preacher's vulnerability and to help students see that professors, too, have their times of spiritual dryness, and need to be thankful on cue.

The heart of the sermon is a retelling in narrative form of the opening section of Paul's Letter to the Philippians. An attempt is made to catch the possible emotions of Paul in his situation, and to show that he maintains a spirit of gratitude to God although he is in prison and faces an uncertain future. Paul is used as an example.

Surely it can't be Thanksgiving already. Why, I am just getting organized for the fall semester, and suddenly it hits me that we have only one more week of classes. Thanksgiving already? But I still have little bags of M & M's and miniature Snickers bars left over from Trick or Treat at Halloween. (I always buy enough to assure a surplus for several weeks.)

One month from today is Christmas Day. Here Christmas is hurtling at me like a runaway train, and somehow I've got to squeeze Thanksgiving in there first. After all, Rich's Great Tree will be lighted two nights from tonight.

There is really no good reason why Thanksgiving should come as such a surprise. It has been on the calendar all the time. We've had to shuffle class schedules to get around it. And yesterday we had an appropriate service of thanksgiving in the chapel.

Perhaps it slips up on us — or at least on me — not so much for chronological reasons as for psychological reasons. I've simply been too preoccupied lately with a variety of concerns to think much about being thankful. I've been principally concerned with survival until the end of term. Or perhaps I've read and heard too many sermons from Job and Ecclesiastes to be happily basking in an upbeat, overly optimistic view of life.

And now, according to the calendar, I am supposed to be thankful on cue. I sometimes have a hard time doing that. Just because Ronald Reagan issues a proclamation that says, "Be thankful," does not guarantee that a warm, cozy glow will immediately well up inside me. To be called upon to be thankful on cue reminds me a little of those times in chapel when we set aside a particular moment when everybody is supposed to smile and hug each other.

I realize that I am being overly cynical here. In resisting being thankful on cue I am perhaps centering too much on whether I feel like being thankful instead of stopping to consider what true gratitude is about. Perhaps the flatness of the pulse of my soul could do with some prodding, some stimulation, to encourage it to pick up its pace.

A designated season of Thanksgiving might well help do that. If I'm not inclined at the moment to be thankful spontaneously, then perhaps I need a celestial stage director or prompter to give me a cue.

As people of God, our spirits are supposed to be turned Godward at all times. But under the weight of our humanness they easily flag, sag, and trail in the dust. From time to time someone needs to come along and say, "Lift up your hearts."

The church has always set aside particular times for its people to gather and offer praise to God. Whether we feel like worshiping may not always coincide with 11:00 on a Sunday morning — or 10:00 on a Tuesday. But the services are not suspended until we

160

can take the spiritual temperature of the expected worshipers. Often these services begin with a call to worship — "Let us worship God." This is almost like saying, "Be thankful on cue."

The Bible itself is replete with exhortations — or perhaps we should call them invitations — to be thankful, to be joyful, to rejoice.

"Enter into God's gates with thanksgiving, and into his courts with praise. Be thankful unto him and bless his name."

"In everything by prayer and supplication, with thanksgiving, let your requests be made known unto God."

And then there is that exuberant exhortation: Rejoice! It is none other than the apostle Paul who writes, "Rejoice in the Lord always, and again I say, 'Rejoice.' " And he writes that from a Roman prison. He writes it from an atmosphere of grave uncertainty — the uncertainty of whether he will ever be released; the uncertainty of whether the outcome of his imprisonment will be life or death.

Have you ever tried to imagine what the remaining hostages in Lebanon must feel? Hopes raised one day to be cruelly dashed the next. Living through the drabness of days that drag endlessly along with no apparent purpose; always facing the possibility of death from capricious captors.

Were I in their situation — or had I been in Paul's — I think I would find it difficult to face a television camera and say with sincerity and confidence, "Rejoice in the Lord always, and again I say, 'Rejoice.' "

But those who have been released give evidence that they were given strength to endure, and Paul's letter from a Roman jail to the Christians at Philippi is evidence that his invitation to rejoice is no shallow one.

That exhortation is not based on the premise that everything is going as Paul would like it to go or as he would have planned it. On the contrary, a great deal in Paul's situation is exactly the opposite of what he would have chosen.

Can you imagine some situations which would be most likely to make Paul shout, "Rejoice!" and to make him feel like giving thanks?

Surely one would want to be free to roam the world without hindrance, to be a restless ambassador, proclaiming his gospel in places where it had not been heard. But Paul languishes in prison, his wings clipped, his feet shackled, his voice echoing off the cold stones of his cell.

Would he welcome a smiling prison visitor who came to say, "Come on, Paul, rejoice"?

If Paul hears in prison that his work is being carried on and that others are proclaiming the gospel which he preached, surely that would make him glad. But suppose he hears — as he does — that some are filling their calendars with speaking engagements and following frantic schedules in order to advance their own reputations and to outdistance Paul in influence and popularity?

Would not this evidence of disunity and division, this mixture of unworthy motives leave a bitter taste in his mouth, depress him, and override the joy he first felt?

Paul awaits the outcome of his trial. Surely it would make him glad to be declared innocent by the Roman authorities, to be vindicated before his accusers, to be assured of a long life so that he could continue his work until he himself decided to lay it down.

But Paul faces the possibility of a death sentence. He lives in the uncertainty of whether and when the blow will fall.

He would be happier with freedom — but he has imprisonment.

He would prefer harmony, unity, mutuality in the preaching of the gospel — but he gets division, tension, jealousy, unworthy motives.

He seems to lean toward choosing life over death — if the choice were really his. But he has to live with uncertainty.

In the face of such circumstances doesn't Paul's "rejoice" sound a little hollow and strained?

Well, let's look again.

His imprisonment. It has become known to those among the praetorian guard that his imprisonment is not for terrorism but for Christ. Paul may not have started in the prison an Association of Christian Praetorian Guards, but at least he had opportunity to reach some people in prison whom he may never otherwise have met.

The rival preachers. Paul couldn't say, "What does it matter if their statistics in the General Assembly minutes outshine mine? If people are hearing and responding to the gospel, what difference does it make if those they hear it from are jerks? What does it matter whose ad is the biggest in the Saturday church page in the *Journal/Constitution*, or whose name is in the boldest type? At least Christ is being proclaimed, and in that I can rejoice."

And the matter of life or death? Paul can say, "While it seems to me more useful for the gospel for me to be released and live, I can leave the outcome, not to the Roman court, but to God. I can be glad and rejoice whichever way it goes with me."

There are positive things for which Paul is thankful in the Philippian letter — the love that lives and grows between himself and his Philippian friends, their practical, generous, kindly care for him, and most of all for the "surpassing worth of knowing Christ Jesus our Lord."

But the striking thing to me about Paul's attitude in this letter is that he does not have to be thankful on cue. He does not have to wait until everything is well ordered, neatly arranged, serene and calm and certain to know genuine joy, to be thankful to God, and to call on others — not as command but as invitation to rejoice.

Paul's secret seems to be that the center of his life and concern is not himself, or his feelings, or his personal circumstances, but that the center of his life is Christ.

"They know my imprisonment is for Christ."

"Christ is preached and in that I rejoice."

"Christ will be honored in my body, whether by life or by death."

So, perhaps the reason I sometimes have a hard time being thankful on cue — or need some specific cue to trigger my gratitude — is that the center of my concern has shifted too far toward me, and that it needs to be tilted back toward the true center of gravity — tilted far enough to where it is possible for even me to say, not simply as a liturgical formula, but as a genuine expression of gratitude to God, "Rejoice in the Lord always, and again I say, 'Rejoice.' "

On Plowing New Ground

This sermon was prepared for and preached at a service in the Columbia Seminary chapel during the first week of the academic year of 1990-91. The Sacrament of the Lord's Supper was celebrated at this service.

The sermon uses the call of Elisha as an analogy of the call to follow Jesus Christ, with special emphasis upon the call to ministry. Many in the congregation were just beginning their seminary training; most of the remainder were people who were also committed to ministry.

The sermon is a retelling of the biblical story with the attempt to reflect the possible emotions of Elisha as he faces the decision to leave his home and follow Elijah. The slaying and sacrificing of the oxen are interpreted in a sacramental way. While not related directly to the sermon, Luke 9:57-62 was read as part of the order of worship. This passage deals with the call of Jesus to follow him. It ends with the saying, "No one who puts a hand to the plow and looks back is fit for the kingdom of God." The allusion to the call of Elisha seems obvious.

It says here that Elisha was plowing with twelve yoke of oxen, and that he was with the twelfth. Now that is a lot of oxen, for a yoke is a pair of two. Two times twelve is 24. Elisha had 24 oxen on that field.

The picture I get from a first glance at this story is of 24 oxen hitched to one plow, and Elisha with the twelfth pair struggling to keep all those oxen going down a straight furrow.

Twenty-four oxen hitched to one plow? What power! He must have been plowing new ground — you know, ground that has not been plowed before, with stumps, roots, and rocks in it. For such ground Elisha would need a 24-ox power machine.

Another thing puzzles me. When he got to the end of the furrow, how would he turn all those oxen around? He would have to make a very wide swath indeed.

And what about the end of the story when it says that Elisha killed the oxen, boiled their flesh, and invited everybody to a big feast? What a stew! What a pot!

Or perhaps it means that there were twelve plows in the field, each hitched to one yoke of oxen, and each guided by a plowman. In that case, I suppose, Elisha would be the boss.

But whatever the arrangement of the oxen, yokes, and plows, Elisha would have his hands full. He was no small-time farmer scratching out a living from one little patch of barren ground. He had twelve yoke of oxen in his field. What one yoke of oxen could plow in a day was the unit of land measurement, like an acre.

Oxen and yokes and plowed fields were the symbols of Elisha's life. I wonder if he did not relish the power which surged through the handles of the plow as he gripped it and followed the plodding oxen down the furrow. I wonder if he did not breathe deep the smell of the freshly turned earth as he plowed new ground and said to himself, "This is good." I suspect that he watched with eager anticipation as the field grew green in spring. And when the harvest came, what joy, what fulfillment, what satisfaction.

If Elisha was breaking up new ground with a 24-ox power tractor then he must have been expanding his holdings. Or if he had twelve plows going at one time he was a big operator. To leave all this and go round the countryside saying to kings and anybody else who did not want to listen, "Thus says the Lord," would call for a radical decision.

And yet one day Elisha had to face that very decision. An old prophet who had been in plenty of trouble with kings and false prophets and wicked queens and who had endured famines and gone through storms and earthquakes came by the field. He waited until Elisha got to the end of the furrow and was trying to figure out how to turn all those oxen around. The passerby threw his cloak over Elisha's shoulders and went on down the road.

(By the way, the old prophet's name was Elijah, so much like Elisha that it is easy to get the two mixed up on a Bible content exam.)

Elisha left his oxen and ran down the road to catch up with Elijah. Now when he overtook him, he did not say, "Sir, you dropped your cloak back there and it fell on my shoulders. Here it is. You might need it when night comes."

Elisha knew that when Elijah threw his mantle over his shoulders that the old man meant for Elisha to follow him and to share his mission and his life. Was he being called to plow a different kind of new ground, or put his hand to a different kind of plow and not look back?

Such a serious decision, such a radical change, such a challenging furrow called for a sacramental act to mark the boundaries between the old and the new, the celebration of a new beginning.

So Elisha took the yokes of oxen and sacrificed them. Their life blood, God's own gift, flowed out before him. I wonder if there was not agony in Elisha's soul as he slew the faithful, innocent beasts. It was a costly sacrifice, a sacrifice for a particular, special occasion. Then he took the wooden yokes rubbed smooth by the muscular shoulders of the laboring oxen and he broke them in pieces and laid the pieces in order. He set them ablaze and the fire from the broken yokes boiled the flesh of the oxen, and a feast was prepared.

The invitation went out: "Come to the table. Share with me the broken symbols of who I was, of who I am becoming. Come, eat and celebrate with me, for I must soon be on the road. Elijah's mantle has touched my shoulders, and it is like a welcomed yoke upon my neck."

They came. The people came, and Elisha gave them the food, and they ate.

The feasting over, Elisha said farewell. He ran and caught up with Elijah. The fertile field, the faithful oxen, the smooth rubbed yokes — I doubt that these were entirely forgotten. But there was within Elisha an irresistible urging to hear a new voice, to take on a different mission, to plow new ground, to put his hand to the plow and not look back.

That is the way it is with the call of God. A mantle brushes our shoulder, but we can still feel its weight after it has been taken away. There is a voice from the road, "Follow me," and the one who calls moves on and we must decide.

Such a decision may well be encouraged, supported, sustained by a sacramental act which celebrates the division between the old and the new, which marks a costly sacrifice that makes a new life possible.

Are we not about to engage in such a sacrament here and now?

Come then, share the meal which has been prepared. Life blood, God's own gift, is poured out. Yokes are broken to make this meal possible. Let us put our hands to the plow and not look back.

Yokes, you say? But one of them looks to me very much like a Cross.

Daniel 2:1-12, 27-28a

Capturing The Butterfly Dream

This sermon was preached in the Columbia Seminary chapel during the summer session of 1992.

The sermon begins with a fanciful story about a man who dreams he is a butterfly, but cannot remember the dream after he awakes. This leads into the biblical narrative of Nebuchadnezzar's dream which he cannot remember but which torments him until he gets an interpretation.

The king and his magicians are made to look ridiculous as the king tries to remember the dream and the magicians are helpless because the king will not tell them what the dream was. Their declaration, "None can tell you the dream, O, King, except the gods whose dwelling is not with flesh" is countered by Daniel's proclamation, "There is a God in heaven who reveals mysteries."

The sermon seeks to expose the powerlessness of human might and wisdom to discover the answers to the mysteries of life, and proposes that the mysteries can only be revealed by God, and that the fullest revelation of God's mystery is in Jesus Christ. The incarnation is proof that God does dwell with flesh; in fact, God dwells in flesh in Jesus.

Once upon a time, a certain man had a strange dream. He dreamed that he was a butterfly. His body felt long and light. He was sure that he had great wings splashed with rippling blue and glimmering gold, bordered with velvet black along the edges. He had only to spread his wings, and he felt himself dipping and soaring, gliding and fluttering in the warm sunlight, riding the crest of a gentle breeze, free and exuberant, buoyant and weightless in an airy heaven which had no limits.

Then he awoke. But the dream had been so real that for several minutes he could not decide whether he was a man dreaming he was a butterfly, or a butterfly dreaming he was a man.

He sat up in bed. He reached out into the pale air and tried to capture the dream, tried to grasp the butterfly which had been himself, tried to touch again the ethereal freedom he had felt. But the butterfly dream slipped through his hands, leaving a bit of glittering dust on his fingertips.

His dream was gone, and he sat there desperately trying to recapture it, reaching for a butterfly and finding his hands dripping with emptiness.

So did King Nebuchadnezzar stir into wakefulness, troubled by a dream which kept trying to break through but which he could not quite recall. It had all seemed so real. He was sure that he would never forget it and would be able to describe it in great detail, including colors. But now in the early morning light it escaped him. He could not quite bring it into focus, and it was driving him mad.

But he was the king, a great king. His word was law. He had only to speak and it was done.

And he had magicians, enchanters, sorcerers. All he had to do was command, "Tell me my dream," and one of his well-paid psychics would paint it with words like a mural upon his palace wall for all to see.

Summon the sorcerers! Bring in the magicians! Gather the enchanters!

"Tell me my dream, and tell me what it means," commands the king.

The sorcerers look at the magicians; the magicians look at the enchanters; the enchanters look at the psychics; and they all look back at the king.

Surely they have not heard the king aright. So together they chant, "O, King, live forever. Tell your servants the dream, and we will show the interpretation."

The king cannot admit that he cannot remember the dream. The wise men have to admit that they cannot interpret a dream that is not told.

170

So the king takes refuge in blustering rage: "Tell me my dream or I will tear you limb from limb!"

The magicians take refuge in admitting that they are a little less wise than the gods: "No one can tell you the dream, O King, except the gods whose dwelling is not with flesh."

So king and magicians alike grasp handfuls of thin air, trying to capture a dream which is as devious and elusive as a butterfly. Its wispy wings brush by and tickle the imperial nose. And the palace is rocked by a majestic sneeze. What can kings and magicians do with butterfly dreams, especially if they believe that only the gods can reveal mysteries, and if they believe that the dwelling of the gods is not with human flesh.

Like a troubled king we human creatures toss upon the bed of our finiteness and grope for a dream which haunts us, but which we cannot seem to grasp. Or bring into focus. Or interpret by our wisdom. Like a butterfly the dream dips and darts before us, and we cannot capture it.

There is an emptiness within us, a longing for an exuberant freedom and joy, a grasping for meaning and purpose, an unspoken, gnawing question: "Is this all there is?"

Mysteries abound compounded by our belief that God is good, for if God is good then why is there evil in the world; why is there suffering and death; why is sin so pervasive and so attractive? I have a feeling that my butterfly dream which I cannot seem to recapture has something to do with questions like these. But try as I might by logic, wisdom, knowledge, philosophies, or technology, the mysteries of the interpretation escape me.

So Nebuchadnezzar's magicians were right! "None can reveal the dream except the gods, whose dwelling is not with flesh."

Or was Daniel right when he said, "There is a God in heaven who reveals mysteries, and he has disclosed ... what will happen at the end of days"?

What this God who reveals mysteries has disclosed at the end of days is that the dwelling of the God of Heaven *is* with flesh.

The same God who troubled the king with dreams seeks to break through the cobwebbed dimness of our souls to make known the mystery of his Will. The dream which long has stirred within the blank spaces of our beings emerges, takes shape, becomes substance, draws near. It is the image of the invisible God; Emmanuel, God with us; the Word becomes flesh and dwells among us!

He shares our journeys. He speaks our language and makes it the vehicle of the Word of God. He weeps our tears. He laughs with us and helps us to laugh at ourselves.

He stoops down to play with a child. He stands tall and blazes with a holy wrath as he wrenches the lash from the slave master's hand and breaks the chains of the slave.

He embraces the leper from whom I doubtless would recoil. He eats with outcasts whose invitation I would politely decline. He calls a rich man down from a tree and surprises him with new ways to use his wealth.

He agonizes in prayer as I cannot seem to do. He looks death in the face, welcomes it, and yet dares to hurl the question into the face of God, which my piety makes me hesitate to ask, "My God, my God, why...?"

Death claims him in the prime of life. He fills a grave as I must some day do. But in a burst of glory beyond my comprehension, the grave is empty, and he walks among us once again, more alive than ever.

The dream for which we have longed is no butterfly dream. It is reality. It is the ultimate mystery at last revealed. It is God not only dwelling *with* flesh, but God dwelling *in* flesh, shown forth in the person of Jesus Christ.

Even so, all our questions are not answered. There is much mystery still. But our feelings about the questions and the mysteries have changed. We can be satisfied with questions which have no absolute answers — yet. We can wait in awe before the mysteries until God's own time. For we know that there is a God in heaven who reveals mysteries, and whose dwelling is with flesh.

We look and see — this is what God is like when God dwells with flesh.

We look and see — this is what you and I are called to be.

Ah. A butterfly just settled on my hand.

I let it loose to rest upon your souls.

(After the words "... are called to be" I began to leave the pulpit; then I stopped, turned to the congregation, held up a hand as if a butterfly had just settled on it. Then I gave an upward gesture with that hand as if I were pushing the butterfly into the air.)

Three More Templates

Both Long and Craddock include the template, Problem/Solution, in their list of standard sermon forms (Long 1989, p. 127; Craddock 1985, p. 177). Since I have already discussed the problem-solution shape of "This Above All," "Thank God And Take Courage," and "A Gift For One Who Has Everything," I will mention only briefly two additional sermons that offer noteworthy variations, "Remember The Loaves" and "Is Confession Too Easy?"

The opening section of "Remember The Loaves" consists of three stories which invite various members of the congregation to identify the sermonic problem in their own lives — a profound sense of inadequacy that can undermine ministry and meaningful living. Ormond explores this problem from the perspective of a seminary student, a supervising pastor, and "an ordinary Christian." The problem emerges: When faced with a crippling sense of inadequacy, what is one to do? At the end of each story Ormond hints at the solution through allusions to bread. Having established the problem by means of the three vignettes, Ormond then turns to the scripture passage and the "answer" it proposes. The sermon's final section applies the solution — bread as memory of divine presence — to the situation of each central character in the opening vignettes. The template is problem/solution; yet how different is this variation from the sermons examined above.

"Is Confession Too Easy?" is a second sermon that exhibits the problem/solution pattern. This sermon begins with an extended personal story that raises the distinction between confession that is genuinely life-changing and confession that is "too easy." It is this extended personal story that sets this version of the problem/solution pattern apart from other examples. The opening story introduces the general theme. Ormond then probes the particular problem of easy confession based on his experiences of seminary chapel services. His hope is that the congregation will recognize the problem and claim it as their own. The problem presented, Ormond explores a resolution — his hope that the assurance of pardon will end with a semicolon and not a period; that is, that genuine confession will result in changed lives. Again, how different is the particular shape of this problem/solution sermon from the others I have clustered in this category.

Another sermon template that Ormond uses repeatedly and well is Then/Now. Long describes this pattern as "This is the historical situation in the text ... these are the meanings for us now" (Long 1989, p. 127). Long writes:

> *In this form, the circumstances of the text are given (e.g. Amos' word to the socioeconomic situation of Israel in the eighth century B.C.E.) followed by the word of the text for today (e.g. Amos' word to our socioeconomic situation). This may be done in two large steps (then/today) or as a series of interweavings (then/today/then/today/then/today).* (Ibid., pp. 127-128)

Long continues:

> *This form is best suited to those texts in which the preacher has identified what James Sanders has called a "dynamic analogy" between the text and the contemporary situation. No historical situation is repeated exactly, but a dynamic analogy results when we identify in some ways with characters or circumstances in the text and thus participate in the tensions and resolutions of the text.* (Ibid., p. 128)

Consistently, Ormond's pattern in this cluster of sermons is Then/Now, or Then/Today, and each sermon turns on one or more points of "dynamic analogy" that link the biblical situation and life today. The sermons that I have put under this category are "A Voice Against The Wind," "Isn't Once Enough?" "When The Wine Fails," and "Three Loaves At Midnight." Although the general pattern is the same, the variations are noteworthy.

"A Voice Against The Wind" and "Isn't Once Enough?" are very similar in shape. The first sentence of both sermons throws the congregation directly into the biblical story, and the first major section of the sermon consists of an imaginative retelling of the story. Ormond states his purpose in retelling the story in his introduction to "A Voice Against The Wind": he hopes

> ... to draw the hearers into the emotions, sights, and sounds of the narrative so that they can identify with the sense of helplessness the disciples felt in the storm as well as the awe and assurance which swept over them when they realized that Jesus had come to them in the midst of the storm.

Similarly, "Isn't Once Enough?" seeks to draw the congregation into Peter's emotions, and, by identification, into their own. In each sermon the retelling of the biblical story dominates the first section of the sermon with only occasional, brief interpretive reflections. In both sermons these reflective asides consist of a parallel with another biblical story (Moses, in one; Jacob, in the other), questions addressed to the text, and implied parallels with emotions or circumstances in the congregation's lives.

When the biblical story has been told, there is a clear shift to the present day: "Perhaps some of you ..." or "Nor am I sure that I am comfortable with him now." Thus begins the Now section with which each sermon ends. The repetition of language and imagery preserves the feel of the initial story. There is no shift from preacher as storyteller to preacher as critical interpreter. Each story continues with the congregation now a character in the biblical story. Like disciples in the boat, the congregation is invited to "look" and "listen." Like Peter, the congregation is invited to feel the uncomfortable persistence of Jesus and then to rejoice in the grace of that same persistence.

"When The Wine Fails" and "Three Loaves At Midnight" present variations on this pattern. Both begin not *in* the biblical story but *looking* at the story. The preacher is not the story's teller but its interpreter. Within a few sentences, however, the interpreter becomes narrator and the story takes over. In the Now section, however, Ormond is less the storyteller and once again the interpreter, returning to the point of view with which the sermon begins. In these two sermons, Ormond in the final section suggests meanings for the sermon's central image — wine, in one; three loaves of bread, in the other.

Six sermons are examples of the final template I will discuss, "Now/Then/Now." Long considers this form a variation of the category "This is the historical situation in the text ... these are the meanings for us now"; the variation makes use of flashback (Long 1989, p. 128). Craddock designates this pattern "the flashback (from present to past to present)" (Craddock 1985, p. 177). What is clear in all six sermons is the segmentation into three distinct sections — Now/Then/Now or Present/Past/Present.

The similarities among "Barefoot In The Pulpit," "A New Day Begins With Breakfast," and "Advent On A Shoestring" are unmistakable and will form the basic template. It is Ormond's personal version of the standard template. First there is an I-section that recounts a true personal story. This section establishes certain motifs around which the sermon will revolve — shoes or no shoes; a new day and breakfast; shoestrings, tying, and untying. In the second section Ormond tells a biblical story, or, in the case of "Advent On A Shoestring," two biblical stories. This retelling highlights the key motifs from the first story. Finally, in a third section Ormond suggests meanings for today that highlight once again the sermon's key motifs and that grow out of the sermon's two previous sections.

Three sermons vary this pattern. "On Being Thankful On Cue" changes the middle section so that it is not a retelling of a single biblical story but rather a portrait of the apostle Paul. In passing, let me mention that this sermon could also be analyzed according to the form discussed above, Problem/Solution. "On Plowing New Ground" and "The Butterfly Dream" vary the first section of the sermon. In "On Plowing New Ground" the initial I-section is not a separate story but a questioning of the text that gradually shades into a retelling of the Elisha story. In "The Butterfly Dream" the opening story is not a personal one but the story of a dream narrated in the third person. The overall pattern in all three, however, is the same: a contemporary story or a viewing of the biblical story from a contemporary vantage point; a flashback to a biblical story or a portrait of a biblical personage; and meanings for "us."

Again, my aim in analyzing these sermons is not to reduce their complexity or limit their richness. My aim is to suggest patterns and possibilities that are options for other preachers and students of preaching. I am convinced that we preachers, like those in the past who aspired to be painters or cathedral builders, can learn the basics and expand the range of our skills by apprenticing ourselves to a preacher like Will Ormond, who knows so well the art of sermon-making.

Notes

1. Eugene L. Lowry makes the distinction between narrative sermons and story-sermons in his Introduction to *How to Preach a Parable: Designs for Narrative Sermons* (Nashville: Abingdon Press, 1989), pp. 13-15.

2. Albert E. Radford, Harry E. Ahles, and C. Ritchie Bell, ed., *Manual of the Vascular Flora of the Carolinas* (Chapel Hill: University of North Carolina Press, 1968), p. xxxxvii.

3. For a description of the differences between the inductive approach of Fred B. Craddock and that of Ralph L. Lewis and Gregg Lewis, see my chapter, "The Parameters of Narrative Preaching," in *Journeys toward Narrative Preaching*, Wayne Bradley Robinson, ed. (New York: Pilgrim Press, 1990), pp. 23-41.

4. For an introduction to story-preaching, see Richard A. Jensen's "Story Preaching," chapter in *Telling the Story: Variety and Imagination in Preaching* (Minneapolis: Augsburg Publishing House, 1980), pp. 114-61, and Bruce C. Salmon's *Storytelling in Preaching: A Guide to the Theory and Practice* (Nashville: Broadman Press, 1988). For an introduction to biblical storytelling, see William J. Bausch's *Storytelling: Imagination and Faith* (Mystic, Connecticut: Twenty-third Publications, 1984). For a deductive approach to story-sermons, see Harold Freeman, *Variety in Biblical Preaching: Innovative Techniques and Fresh Forms* (Waco, Texas: Word Books, Word Inc., 1987).

5. See David Buttrick, *Homiletic: Moves and Structures* (Philadelphia: Fortress Press, 1987).

6. This approach to analyzing a text, in this case a sermon, from the reader's or receiver's point of view is called Reader-Response Criticism. The critic looks for clues that indicate the response the text seeks to create in the reader. I am applying this method to sermons here and asking, "In a sermon what is the effect of the inductive approach and the deductive approach on the congregation as receivers of the sermon as text?" See Robert M. Fowler, *Let the Reader Understand: Reader-Response Criticism and the Gospel of Mark* (Minneapolis: Fortress Press, 1991). Or see Fowler's chapter, "Reader-Response Criticism: Figuring Mark's Reader," in *Mark and Method: New Approaches in Biblical Studies,*

Janice Capel Anderson and Stephen D. Moore, ed. (Minneapolis: Fortress Press, 1992). See also Edgar V. McKnight, *Post-Modern Use of the Bible: The Emergency of Reader-Oriented Criticism* (Nashville: Abingdon, 1988). For a critique of this method as it is practiced by biblical scholars, see Stephen D. Moore, "Stories of Reading: Doing Gospel Criticism as/with a Reader," chapter in *Literary Criticism and the Gospels: The Theoretical Challenge* (New Haven: Yale University Press, 1989), pp. 71-107. Thomas G. Long combines a reader-response method and a rhetorical method of reading scripture with preaching in *Preaching and the Literary Forms of the Bible* (Philadelphia: Fortress Press, 1989).

7. This is the goal of inductive preaching according to *Inductive Preaching: Helping People Listen*, by Ralph L. Lewis with Gregg Lewis (Westchester, Illinois: Crossway Books, Good News Publishers, 1983).

8. Eugene L. Lowry is the primary champion of narrative preaching as it differs from story-preaching. See his books *The Homiletical Plot: The Sermon as Narrative Art Form* (Atlanta: John Knox Press, 1980); *Doing Time in the Pulpit: The Relationship Between Narrative and Preaching* (Nashville: Abingdon Press, 1985); and *How to Preach A Parable: Designs for Narrative Sermons* (Nashville: Abingdon Press, 1989). See also his chapter, "The Narrative Quality of Experience as a Bridge to Preaching," in *Journeys toward Narrative Preaching*, Wayne Bradley Robinson, ed. (New York: Pilgrim Press, 1990), pp. 67-77, and his essay, "The Revolution of Sermonic Shape" in *Listening to the Word: Studies in Honor of Fred B. Craddock*, ed. Gail R. O'Day and Thomas G. Long (Nashville: Abingdon Press, 1993), pp. 93-112.

9. This is Aristotle's definition of a plot in *The Poetics (Aristotle, vol. 23, The Poetics; "Longinus," On the Sublime; Demetrius, On Style*, Loeb Classical Library, ed. G. P. Goold [Cambridge: Harvard University Press, 1982]). See section 7:2-7.

10. See Fred B. Craddock, *Preaching* (Nashville: Abingdon, 1985), pp. 162-165, for a description of the role of identification in preaching.

11. This pattern of No/No/Yes is itself a template that can shape an entire sermon. Craddock (1985, p. 177) and Long (1989) both include this pattern in their list of sermon forms. Craddock's version is "Not this, nor this, nor this, nor this, but this" (1985, p. 177).

12. See Katherine Paterson for her description of "a proper ending" ("Hope and Happy Endings," chapter in *The Spying: More Thoughts on Reading and Writing for Children* [New York: Lodestar Books, E. P. Dutton, 1989], pp. 172-191). She describes her endings as "rooted in this earth and leaning in the direction of the New Jerusalem" (p. 191). See Eugene L. Lowry for his understanding of a resolution rooted in the gospel (1980, pp. 37, 83; 1985, pp. 24, 66).

Works Cited

Craddock, Fred B. 1979. *As One without Authority: Essays on Inductive Preaching*. 3rd ed. Nashville: Abingdon Press.

_____. 1985. *Preaching*. Nashville: Abingdon Press.

Lewis, Ralph L., with Gregg Lewis. 1983. *Inductive Preaching: Helping People Listen*. Westchester, Illinois: Crossway Books.

Long, Thomas G. 1989. *The Witness of Preaching*. Louisville, Kentucky: Westminster/John Knox Press.

Lowry, Eugene L. 1985. *Doing Time in the Pulpit: The Relationship between Narrative and Preaching*. Nashville: Abingdon Press.

Paterson, Katherine. 1981. *Gates of Excellence: On Reading and Writing Books for Children*. New York: Elsevier/Nelson Books.

_____. 1989. *The Spying Heart: More Thoughts on Reading and Writing Books for Children*. New York: Lodestar Books, E. P. Dutton.